Parapsychology and Religion

Religion and Psychology

Volumes published in this Brill Research Perspective are listed at *brill.com/rpsys*

Parapsychology and Religion

By

Everton de Oliveira Maraldi

BRILL

LEIDEN | BOSTON

Library Congress Control Number: 2021907434

Typeface for the Latin, Greek, and Cyrillic scripts: "Brill". See and download: brill.com/brill-typeface.

ISSN 2772-2619
ISBN 978-90-04-46567-1 (paperback)
ISBN 978-90-04-46783-5 (e-book)

Printed by Printforce, United Kingdom

Contents

Parapsychology and Religion

Everton de Oliveira Maraldi
Pontifical Catholic University of São Paulo, Brazil
everton.nom@gmail.com

Abstract

"Parapsychology and religion" is perhaps the most controversial research area in the psychology of religion. Initially, psychology and parapsychology were not distinct disciplines but later dissociated as a result of the boundary-work carried out to establish the former as a natural science. In recent decades, the psychology of religion has witnessed a growing literature bearing on ontological issues including parapsychological topics such as distant healing and near-death experiences. In this work, it is argued that despite the methodological and theoretical controversies that still surround the field of parapsychology, the findings of research on alleged anomalous processes merit serious scientific examination. More specifically, this work explores how parapsychological findings may inform research on religious/spiritual experiences. It begins with a brief review of the history of psychical research / parapsychology, pointing out its connections with the development of modern psychology and the circumstances that have set these research fields apart. After discussing some fundamental terminological and conceptual issues in parapsychology and psychology, the psychological literature on the paranormal is critically reviewed, arguing that over time it became less of a scientific endeavor and more of an ideological program devised to denigrate paranormal believers and experiencers. It is then shown how an informed, open-minded dialogue between parapsychology and psychology of religion might help us move beyond the present ideological disputes in favor of a unified perspective. A shift from belief to experience is defended and both the strengths and limitations of the latter are discussed, showing how parapsychology responds to such limitations through systematic observation and experimentation. The complex relations between parapsychology and religion over time are also reviewed, surveying the variety of perspectives embraced by parapsychologists in this regard and their implications for an understanding of religious experience and spirituality.

Keywords

parapsychology – religion – spirituality – paranormal – psychology

1   Introduction

By the late 19th and early 20th centuries, the Spiritualist movement had spread throughout the United States and Europe. Reports of spirit communication through 'mediums' – individuals believed to serve as intermediaries between the living and the dead – abounded and spiritualist séances were widely attended, mainly for leisure. But some became convinced that there was more to them than entertainment and that spiritualist phenomena had moral and philosophical implications as well. Many philosophies and religious movements had emerged out of Victorian spiritualism, of which Spiritism in France and the "Harmonial Philosophy" of the American spiritualist Andrew Jackson Davis (1826–1910) are some illustrative examples (Podmore, 1902; Doyle, 1926; Aubrée and Laplantine, 1990).

At the time, experimental psychology was in its infancy, struggling to distance itself from philosophy and achieve recognition as a natural science. The lay public, though, was unaware of such developments and often conflated psychology with the study of spiritual phenomena (Coon, 1992). Less often acknowledged, however, is that accounts of psychic occurrences also attracted much attention from the founding fathers of psychology such as William James (1842–1910), Théodore Flournoy (1854–1920), and Carl Gustav Jung (1875–1961). In fact, the investigation of paranormal experiences played a crucial role in the initial development of research on unconscious processes, hallucinations, dissociation, hypnosis, eyewitness testimony, and false memories (Alvarado, 2002; 2020; Cardeña, 2018; Maraldi and Alvarado, 2018).

Flournoy, James, and Jung saw mediumship as a via regia to the unconscious, much like Sigmund Freud (1856–1939) conceived of dreams. They argued that the investigation of trance mediums and their descriptions of a spiritual world had the potential to shed light on a series of psychological phenomena still poorly understood from dissociative identity disorder (formerly called "multiple personality") to creativity and imagination (Shamdasani, 1994; Maraldi and Alvarado, 2018). But beyond these psychological matters, they also maintained a serious scientific interest in the investigation of psychic phenomena claimed by spiritualist mediums and even helped to establish what was then a new scientific discipline entirely devoted to the investigation of paranormal claims, the field of *psychical research*. In 1882, a group of scholars from Cambridge founded in London the Society for Psychical Research (or SPR), the first organization dedicated to such studies. In 1884, William James helped found the American Society for Psychical Research, and in 1894, he served as president of the London SPR.

Although representing a wide variety of scholarly fields, ranging from literature to physics, the members of the Society had in common the project of investigating "without prejudice and prepossession of any kind" and "in the same spirit of exact and unimpassioned inquiry which has enabled Science to solve so many problems", a "large group of debatable phenomena designated by such terms as mesmeric, psychical, and Spiritualistic" which are "inexplicable on any generally recognized hypothesis" (SPR, 1883). Among these "debatable phenomena" were alleged telepathy (in which specific information is apparently and somehow directly transferred from one mind to another), physical phenomena associated with Spiritualism (e.g., alleged materializations of spirits of the deceased), reports of apparitions at the moment of death, reportedly haunted houses, and 'mesmerism' (a term used to define a broad range of alternative medical practices and conceptions which antedated contemporary theories of hypnosis, suggestion, and the placebo response), named so in reference to the work of German physician Franz Anton Mesmer (1734–1815).

As one could expect, these investigations were strongly influenced by their historical and social milieu and the prevailing spiritual beliefs. Among the philosophical-religious issues that usually concerned the pioneers of psychical research was the possibility of an afterlife. In his introduction for one of SPR's most prominent works, *Phantasms of the Living*, the main theoretician among the members of the Society, Frederic Myers (1843–1901), poet and professor of classical literature, established a direct relationship between the scientific findings concerning psychic phenomena and the validity of religious beliefs: "if our evidence to recent supernormal occurrences be discredited, a retrospective improbability will be thrown on much of the content of religious tradition" (Gurney, Myers and Podmore, 1886, p. XII). For him, these experiences – after excluding cases of fraud, deception, self-deception, and other methodological shortcomings – were real and demonstrated the existence of an immaterial or transcendent aspect of human personality (Myers, 1903). In his vision, phenomena such as telepathy and clairvoyance in which specific information is somehow directly obtained by the individual concerning distant (and sometimes obscure) events, such as lost people or distant locations, were "survivals from the powers which that spirit once exercised in a transcendental world" (Myers, 1903, Vol. 2, p. 267).

But there were other psychologists and academics at the time who took a very different perspective from that of Myers and emphasized an eminently negative, psychopathological view of mediumship, combined with a combative approach to Spiritualism. Among these were James McKeen Cattell (1860–1944), Hugo Münsterberg (1863–1916), Joseph Jastrow (1863–1944), and Stanley

Hall (1846–1924). In their view, the involvement of eminent psychologists with psychical research could ruin the establishment of psychology as a scientific discipline. As Pence explains (2020, p. 1):

> For advocates like William James, the question was one of open-mindedness – a good empiricist would hear the case out, following the evidence wherever it led. For opponents like James Cattell, they represented a serious threat. To openly discuss such matters risked lending credibility to popular irrationalism and the hucksters preying on it.

Sommer (2012) argues that these early efforts to debunk claims of spiritualist phenomena comprised good examples of what he calls *boundary-work*. When Hall (1909) explained several of these phenomena in terms of fraud, deception or hallucinations, he aimed to draw a clear line between psychology and psychical research. In fact, it was his opinion that a research field devoted to the study of psychic phenomena was not necessary, since psychology alone was sufficient to explain seemingly paranormal occurrences based on the knowledge provided by the investigation of natural, psychological processes (Alvarado, 2014).

But this was not without some ambiguity and concession. Coon (1992, p. 146) notes, for example, that despite being contrary to spiritualist beliefs, some psychologists of that period investigated cases of mediums with the aim of obtaining funding for research.

> [...] some of the early funding for psychology laboratories was provided by citizens interested in supporting psychic research. At Clark University, Hall was embarrassed when the first major bequest – some $5,000 – given to the university for psychological research in 1906 was specifically tagged for research into spiritualism. The archival correspondence between Hall and the estate's lawyer reveals Hall delicately asking if the term "spiritualism" could be left out of the wording of the bequest.

Hall would subsequently publish, together with psychologist Amy Tanner (1870–1956), a book on the case of the medium Leonora Piper (1857–1950), having offered a critical analysis of her trance phenomena (Tanner, 1910).

But even among those who entertained the possibility of real psychic occurrences, not all phenomena were accepted as valid. Notwithstanding his deep interest in the study of mediumship, Flournoy (1911) was skeptical about spirit communication. Nevertheless, he conceded that the medium Hélène Smith, whose spiritual experiences he analyzed in detail in his classic study *Des Indes à lá planéte Mars* ('From India to the Planet Mars') (Flournoy, 1900, p. 415), evidenced some telepathy and psychokinesis – the purported direct influence of mind on matter, such as reports of table levitation without a mechanical or other established scientific explanation. Similarly, Sigmund Freud, who is widely known for depicting religious beliefs as illusions, eventually came to address the possibility of telepathy in works such as 'Psychoanalysis and Telepathy' (1921/1953a) and 'Dreams and Telepathy' (1922/1953b). Flournoy and Freud did not seem to fit a simple categorization of skeptic or believer. Their opinions could vary according to the phenomenon in question and their interpretation of the empirical evidence (Evrard et al., 2017). In effect, Flournoy would be better defined today as an advocate of methodological agnosticism (Porpora, 2006; Murken, 2019) and was cautious about considering evidence for psychic phenomena as necessary proofs of the veracity of religious beliefs.

In *Les Principes de la Psychologie Religieuse*, Flournoy (1903) had postulated the 'Principle of the Exclusion of the Transcendent' according to which psychologists should limit their investigations to the psychological factors involved in religious experiences, without asking themselves about the veracity of the feeling of a divine presence described by the experiencer. The existence of God or a divine realm is always an open possibility, although it should remain outside the purview of psychology. With that principle, Flournoy wished to defend psychology from two main dangers. The first is to be used by religious believers to corroborate their beliefs. The second is the exact opposite to the first, that is, to serve the interests of intellectuals and skeptics who wish to attack and denigrate religion, what would represent, in his own words, an "anti-religious dogma" (Flournoy, 1903, p. 21). For Flournoy, James, and others like Edwin Starbuck (1866–1947), religious experiences are ultimately rooted in our biology and their study can shed light on the nature of the human mind, regardless of their theological and mystical implications. This was in accordance with another of Flournoy's principles, that of the biological interpretation: religious experiences are natural phenomena subjected to the same evolutionary mechanisms underlying other physiological processes. The two interrelated principles – the exclusion of the transcendent and the biological interpretation – paved the way for the development of a scientific psychology of religion, autonomous in relation to theology and philosophy. According to Murken (2019, p. 42), the exclusion of the transcendent "when it was observed, contributed to the success of the psychology of religion in the 20th century".

But besides his two psychological principles, Flournoy also coined two other "axioms" that he believed should guide all investigations of psychic phenomena: the 'Principle of Hamlet', which can be condensed in the expression 'anything is possible', and the 'Principle of Laplace', which can be synthetized in this sentence: "the weight of the evidence should be proportioned to the strangeness of the facts" (Flournoy, 1990, p. 345). According to Flournoy, these two principles are equally valid and interdependent: they balance each other out. The Principle of Hamlet – inspired by the famous play by William Shakespeare (1564–1616) in which Hamlet, the prince, devised a test to determine whether the ghost of his father was real and whether the information conveyed by the ghost was accurate – represents an openness to new facts and possibilities, which is of fundamental importance to the development of science. However, if taken too far, this principle might lead to the irresponsible and thoughtless acceptance of all kinds of allegations. On the other hand, the Principle of Laplace – so named in reference to the mathematician and physicist Pierre Simon Laplace (1749–1827) – demands caution towards evidence or ideas that seem to contradict established theories, especially if those theories have years of evidence in their favor and have many times proved to be useful. Science is not just about advancing new pathways; it is also about accumulating and preserving knowledge. But when exaggerated, the Principle of Laplace turns into a dogmatic reluctance to leave or reformulate established theories and held beliefs.

Flournoy sought to establish a clear delimitation between psychology and metaphysics while at the same time maintaining a serious interest in the study of claims of exceptional phenomena with implications for the legitimacy of religious beliefs, as his four principles illustrate. Taves (2014, p. 377) explains that despite the "division of academic labor between psychology and metaphysics, most researchers [at the turn of the 20th century] nonetheless presumed some sort of connection between the experiences they studied and the 'extraordinary'". However, the later representants of the field largely abandoned the study of psychic experiences, and not without reason since this move might have facilitated wider scientific acceptance.

In the first decades of the 20th century, the program to establish psychology as a scientific field had progressed. New areas and objects of study took the lead, such as childhood and developmental psychology, behaviorism, and psychoanalysis (Coon, 1992; Schultz and Schultz, 2011). Initially, the course taken was not exactly that of the methodological exclusion of the transcendent combined with a psychological interest in the study of religion, as Flournoy had envisaged, but that of an outright rejection of religion, which was often depicted in a negative, psychopathological light. This scenario would only change decades later, especially from the second half of the 20th century when the psychology of religion initiated a new renaissance (Hood Jr., 2012; Wulff, 1991).

Although some psychologists of religion later returned to the subject of the paranormal (e.g., Oesterreich, 1921, 1930; Thouless, 1971), the subsequent investigation of psychic experiences followed a different pathway. The field of psychical research acquired a new name: parapsychology – a term first introduced by the German philosopher Max Dessoir (1867–1947) and later popularized by Joseph Banks Rhine (1895–1980) and psychologist William McDougall (1871–1938). The early impressionistic studies with mediums gave way to standardized experimental tests in which anyone could participate, not only alleged psychics. The use of more rigorous methodological controls against fraud and other 'normal' explanations – such as sensory leakage, selective reporting and artifacts derived from data analysis – increased with time, and the ways of evaluating the evidence now largely parallel those of mainstream science. Parapsychologists have actually collaborated with the creation and development of important scientific methods, such as meta-analysis (Cardêna et al., 2015), registered reports (Wiseman, Watt and Kornbrot, 2019), randomization and masked designs (Hacking, 1988; Cardêna et al., 2015; Watt and Wiseman, 2002). Today, parapsychological experiments often address conventional physical, biological, and psychological explanations for reports of anomalous occurrences. But the controversy surrounding the scientific legitimacy of parapsychology remains and the field continues to be classified by many as an instance of pseudoscience (e.g., Reber and Alcock, 2020; Bunge, 1987, 2010; Spitz, 1997).

This negative portrayal of parapsychology by mainstream scientists is not new and some of the same old arguments are still used by contemporary critics. For example, James was often accused to be naïve and credulous in his analyses of phenomena attributed to Leonora Piper, the medium known for being his 'white crow' – an incomparable case of purportedly supernormal abilities. He and other members of the SPR, such as Myers, Edmund Gurney (1847–1888) and Richard Hodgson (1855–1905) were depicted by critics as obsessed with demonstrating life after death in order to communicate with deceased loved ones (e.g., Cattell, 1896; Tanner, 1910; Hall, 1964; Spitz, 1997). But this argument obscures the variety of perspectives embraced by parapsychologists over time (Tart, 2003), as well as the cases of research collaboration between skeptics and parapsychologists (e.g., Hyman and Honorton,1986; Schiltz, Wiseman, Watt and Radin, 2006). If taken seriously, such *ad hominem* argument could cast doubt on much of the research carried in other scientific fields as well, including the psychology of religion where many researchers have a religious background (e.g., Belzen, 2012).

Another common criticism is that the first psychical researchers neglected evidence against the existence of psychic phenomena while favoring evidence in their support (Spitz, 1997). However, there were many occasions where psychical researchers contested claims of psychic abilities, as illustrated by SPR's report (1885) on the alleged supernormal phenomena reputed to Madame Blavatsky (1831–1891) and the theosophical society. One of the main contributions of early researchers was the exposure of fraudulent mediums and their tricks, which can be observed in several publications of the time (e.g., Carrington, 1908; Podmore, 1897). The founders of psychical research were aware of the limitations of eyewitness testimony – such as incorrect observation and memory and perceptual biases – and searched for ways to test their assumptions more rigorously (Lang, 1909; Knapp, 2017; Pence, 2020). Although much of these early investigations may appear exploratory in view of future developments, it is simply incorrect to classify them as flawed and naïve. Despite the deep interest manifested by Flournoy, Freud, James, and Jung on the ontological status of paranormal claims, their views should not be confused with that of spiritualists and other religious believers. As Knapp explains (2017, p. 4) concerning James:

> James was neither a skeptic nor a debunker. He did not belong to an informal but growing network of self-proclaimed doubters and critics bent on proving Spiritualists' claims false and on exposing mediums as clever charlatans, though he certainly spent a great deal of time separating the frauds and fakers from the genuine subjects worthy of study. His purpose, then, was neither to advance a religious cause nor to undermine one but rather to understand and hypostatize psychic phenomena.

The psychologist Gardner Murphy (1895–1979) shows us how James's attitude toward psychical research seemed to have been significantly shaped by his upbringing and family relationships, evidencing the free-thinking mindset where he was educated:

> In the home environment, one did not laugh at the claims of Swedenborg.[1] One studied them, played with them, tossed them about, rejected some aspects of them, took other aspects more seriously, just as one did with regard to Christian Science, or any of the other new winds of doctrine that swept through the intellectual atmosphere. Questions about telepathy or survival were just as reasonable as any other kind of question. Such questions were not to be decided *a priori*, or in differential regard for authority, but by recourse to rigorous investigation. When, therefore,

---

1   Emanuel Swedenborg (1688–1772) was a Swedish mystic and philosopher considered to have played an important role in the subsequent development of the spiritualist movement (Doyle, 1926).

the Society for Psychical Research was founded in London in 1882 [...] he shared warmly in the whole enterprise.
MURPHY AND BALLOU, 1960, p. 14

Over more than a century, the findings of parapsychological research have been published in a series of mainstream scientific journals – attracting the interest, as well as the disdain and criticism of some mainstream scientists – including *Nature* (e.g., Pratt et al., 1968; Targ and Puthoff, 1974), *American Journal of Psychiatry* (Ullman and Krippner, 1970), *Journal of Nervous and Mental Disease* (e.g., Stevenson, 1977; Daher et al., 2017), *Behavioral and Brain Sciences* (Rao and Palmer, 1987), *Journal of the Royal Society of Medicine* (Hodges and Scofield, 1995), *Journal of Personality and Social Psychology* (Bem, 2011), *American Psychologist* (Cardeña, 2018), among many others. Parapsychologists maintain that the effects they study have been consistently replicated by different researchers, even when the studies accounted for previous methodological flaws (Utts, 1991; Cardeña, 2018). Several eminent scientists and thinkers including some Nobel Prize winners took the possibility of psychic phenomena seriously and even contributed with scientific investigations on this subject, among them Charles Richet (1850–1935), Henri Bergson (1859–1941), Marie Curie (1867–1934), Wolfgang Pauli (1900–1958), and John Eccles (1903–1997) – for a complete list, see Cardeña (2015). The Parapsychological Association, one of the most important international organizations engaged in the study of psychic experiences has been an affiliated organization of the American Association for the Advancement of Science (AAAS) since 1969.

Still, none of these accomplishments had significantly altered parapsychology's status as a marginal science. The field faces many problems, such as lack of funding, few academic departments, unattractive career prospects, and inability to institute and maintain longitudinal studies (Walach et al., 2009; Cardeña et al., 2015). Parapsychologists are still looking for a guiding, integrative theory, capable of sufficiently explaining their experimental findings and directing future research, while some critics still complain about the lack of consistent and ostensible results in favor of paranormal phenomena (e.g., Reber and Alcock, 2020; Bunge, 1987, 2010; Spitz, 1997) – see Irwin and Watt (2007) for a review of such criticisms.

1.1   *Aims of This Work*

Hood et al. (2018) have identified "religion and parapsychology as perhaps the most controversial research area in the psychology of religion" (p. 369). Even though some psychologists do not evidence a combative agenda against parapsychology, they nevertheless refrain from investigating paranormal claims, maintaining a strictly psychological perspective (e.g., Mathijsen, 2009). However, in recent decades, psychology of religion has witnessed a growing interest in ontological issues including parapsychological topics such as inter- cessory prayer and near-death experiences (Miller, 2012; Murken, 2019; Watson, 2019). A similar tendency is also observed in the social sciences (e.g., Bowie, 2014; Hunter, 2015; Kripal, 2017).

I argue that despite the methodological and theoretical controversies that still surround the field of parapsychology, the findings of research on alleged anomalous processes merit serious scientific examination. More specifically, I show how parapsychological research may inform our understanding of reli- gious/spiritual experiences by fostering a more sensible perspective toward the explanations offered by religious and paranormal believers and experi- encers. My aim in this monograph is to exercise the same open-mindedness that guided the work of the first psychologists of religion by *entertaining* the possibility of anomalous phenomena without necessarily *endorsing* it, as also suggested by Schooler et al. (2018). In this regard, I defend that contem- porary psychological research on paranormal beliefs became less a scientific endeavor and more an ideological program devised to denigrate paranormal believers and experiencers. In parts two and three, I explore the conceptual and methodological caveats of these studies and, in part four, I discuss how an informed dialogue between parapsychology and psychology of religion might help us move beyond the present ideological disputes. I defend a research par- adigm where the many existing views are invited to enter the debate, provided a way of scientifically testing their assumptions and without abandoning psy- chology's fundamental purpose which is to study "subjectivity and behavior" (American Psychological Association, 2015, p. 860).

This open-minded view is in accordance with Watson's (2019, p. 5) sugges- tion "that all arguments deserve to be read and submitted to thoughtful dialog- ical consideration". Watson assumes that a neutral psychological perspective is ultimately unattainable, and that psychologists should therefore take into con- sideration the possibility that people's beliefs refer to existing objects. Many authors suggest that beliefs in psychic phenomena are not inherently irra- tional and abstract but are grounded on experience (e.g., Roe, 2020; Hufford, 1982; McClenon, 2002). Although explanations based on personal experience alone are scientifically less reliable and subject to distortion, this cannot serve as a justification to rule out *a priori* the possibility of real psychic processes. As Hufford (1982, p. xviii) importantly remarked:

> ... some significant portion of traditional supernatural belief is associ- ated with accurate observations interpreted rationally. This does not

suggest that *all* such belief has this association. Nor is this association taken as proof that the beliefs are true. This latter point must be stressed because much of the investigation of supernatural belief, especially since the Enlightenment, has been implicitly governed by a desire to show that the beliefs under investigation are false. The easiest way to do this seems to have been to assert that believers lack an understanding of how to separate true propositions from false ones. This has ranged from statements about a lack of appreciation for the rules of logic to assertions that the believer fails to use, at least within the domain of belief, adequate reality testing.

Experiences deemed as psychic, paranormal, supernormal or anomalous (we shall return to the terminological differences and similarities between these terms in part two) are reported worldwide by people from all socioeconomic levels and their narratives of such experiences may sometimes evidence remarkable phenomenological and cross-cultural consistency (Maraldi and Krippner, 2019; McClenon, 2002). The relationship of these experiences with psychopathological indicators is complex (Kerns et al., 2014), but many studies evidence a positive association with well-being and mental health variables, suggesting that a psychopathological interpretation cannot be generalized to all accounts of paranormal experience (e.g., Roxburgh and Roe, 2011; Kennedy, 1994).

Even though I entertain the possibility of real anomalous processes, it is not my purpose in this monograph to advocate in favor of specific theories or hypotheses concerning their nature, nor to propose a new theory. As already pointed out, no theory of psychic phenomena has hitherto achieved wide acceptance or consensus among parapsychologists and the debate regarding the legitimacy of psychic occurrences was not exhausted. My main concerns here are to discuss how parapsychological findings might contribute to a deeper understanding of religious beliefs and experiences, and whether a dialogue between parapsychology and psychology of religion is possible.

By pushing the epistemological boundaries of psychology of religion, I seek to show that there are ontological issues worth considering and that we cannot completely avoid them in scientific research. The consideration of psychic phenomena (or merely of their possibility) could lead psychologists of religion to rethink the generalizability of what I call the *principle of analogy*, that is, the tendency with which theories of religion favor naturalist explanations grounded on analogies with other sociopsychological phenomena instead of considering the explanations offered by the religious experiencers themselves. Based on this principle, religious experiences have been variously defined as symbolic representations of society (Durkheim, 1912), phenomena analogous to neurotic or other psychopathological symptoms (Freud, 1907/1924), or by-products of basic cognitive mechanisms (Boyer, 1994), but only rarely as valid descriptions of genuine processes or events (Lang, 1909). On other hand, parapsychologists seek precisely to evaluate whether reports of psychic phenomena have any ontological basis beyond established psychological, physical, or biological processes. Instead of constantly reiterating the fallibility of human perception and judgement, parapsychologists take people's experiences and interpretations seriously and learn from them – and the spiritual traditions that emerged out of them – to develop their research protocols and theories. If their findings have any validity, this indicates that our psychological theories are incomplete. An adequate understanding of parapsychological findings requires interdisciplinary work. In this regard, psychology of religion can play an important role in this debate, both because of the inspiration of the founding fathers and the profound interrelation between religious and paranormal experiences, as I shall detail in the next parts.

All this discussion concerning the rationality and soundness of psychic experiences might lead some readers to think that I am preparing the ground to affirm, some pages later, that since these experiences are not necessarily irrational or pathological, they should be seen as legitimate evidence of anomalous phenomena and, by extension, of the veracity of religious beliefs. Indeed, some of the fundamental teachings of religions are based on anomalous experiences reported by their founders and practitioners from prophetic dreams to reports of anomalous cures (Taves, 2009). The first psychologists of religion believed that such extraordinary experiences comprise the very essence of religion and the main object of the psychology of religion (e.g., Flournoy, 1902; James, 1920/2002). Many other scholars also recognized the importance of parapsychology to the study of religion (e.g., Lang, 1909; Griffin, 1997; Bowie, 2014; Kripal, 2010, 2017). Following this rationale, if the findings of parapsychology are reliable and confirm that certain religious phenomena are genuine, then parapsychology may help us understand the origins of religion (McClenon, 2002). However, things are more complicated than this.

Parapsychological findings may or may not benefit a spiritual interpretation. As we shall discuss with more detail in part four, parapsychology may actually serve to foster naturalist (though controversial) explanations of psychic experiences (Sudre, 1956). For example, many authors have suggested that these experiences are subjected to biological evolution much in the same way as other neurophysiological and psychological processes (e.g., Broughton, 2015; McClenon, 2002; Stanford, 2015). Others like Braude (1997) have suggested that psychic functioning is best explained by psychoanalytic and secular humanist perspectives rather than divine intervention. Even when findings are apparently congruent with a non-materialist perspective, they may partially contradict established beliefs, as exemplified by investigations of children who claim to remember previous lives. The patterns and characteristics of alleged past-life memories have sometimes contested traditional beliefs about reincarnation such as the existence of karma (Stevenson, 1966/1980). Similarly, some researchers have questioned the existence of an afterlife by arguing that psychic functioning is sufficient to explain apparent spirit communication (see Rock, 2014 for a review of the controversies surrounding the survival hypothesis). These examples show that the relationship between parapsychology and religion can be more ambiguous than usually assumed.

In this sense, parapsychology cannot be simplistically stereotyped as religion disguised as science – as some critics have suggested (e.g., Alcock, 1981, 1987; Bunge, 1991; Spitz, 1997). Instead of unifying all religions in a superordinated, rational system of thought (as often attempted by representants of New Age spirituality), parapsychology may in fact boost disbelief and skepticism, even if unintended. Parapsychology is a daring, frontier endeavor designed to submit religious and other exceptional claims to scientific scrutiny, which means such claims can be contradicted. Historically, parapsychology can be defined as a child of secularization. For some, it is the announcer of a secular or postmodern spirituality (Griffin, 1997; Tart, 2002; 2009; Walach, 2015; Walach et al., 2009). In part four, I explore further whether parapsychology has a spiritual goal and what are the implications of parapsychological findings for the study of religion and spirituality.

All this discussion concerning ontological issues invariably leads us to ask whether parapsychology can really demonstrate or refute, on a fundamental level, the claims of religions, and what are its limitations. Some of the fundamental tenets of religions might be beyond any possible scientific understanding, even if we adopt a different research paradigm, more open to non-materialist (or 'post-materialist') assumptions (Beauregard et al., 2014). What are the questions that parapsychology can answer when religious/spiritual claims are theoretically considered and experimentally examined? Thouless (1971, p. 80) once remarked that "No experimental study [...] can deal directly with the central elements of religious faith: the existence of God, the duty of love, or the meaningfulness of human life, although there are a number of other questions of concern to religious thought on which psychical research can be expected to throw light." These "other questions" are addressed throughout the parts of this monograph.

To conclude the introduction, another important remark is in order. Given the scientific controversy surrounding parapsychological research, some authors feel the need to review all the relevant literature and defend the reliability of the studies presented. However, this monograph was not written to convince the reluctant skeptic nor to bring those on the fence to the side of parapsychology. For more than a century, psychic experiences have been researched and debated, and many authors have dedicated their time and efforts to rigorously examine the most convincing evidence available. My review of the literature is thus not exhaustive but aims to provide the reader with the necessary context and information to follow the discussion and see for herself/himself whether a dialogue between parapsychology and psychology of religion is in any way fruitful or sterile. For those interested in learning more about parapsychological research, the following list of references is a good way forward (Radin, 1997, 2006; Cardeña et al., 2015, May and Marwaha, 2015; Barušs and Mossbridge, 2017).

I am in a peculiar position to carry out this endeavor, for I have scientifically contributed to both areas (e.g., Maraldi et al., 2011; Maraldi et al., 2014; Maraldi, 2017; Maraldi et al., 2017; Lange et al., 2018; Maraldi and Krippner, 2019; Maraldi, 2020; Maraldi and Farias, 2020). As a psychologist, I was trained to identify psychopathological indicators and provide psychological and social explanations for diverse human experiences and behaviors. But as someone raised in a spiritualist environment and native of Brazil, a highly religious country where belief in paranormal phenomena is widespread (Maraldi and Farias, 2020), I remained always curious about the possibility of real psychic occurrences. Today, I am not a spiritualist anymore, but my upbringing has long since made me open to the many explanatory possibilities for accounts of psychic experiences. Thus, this monograph should be read not as the testimony of a convinced believer, but as an effort to present and critically examine the parallels I have been identifying between these two areas of knowledge for more than ten years of investigations.

2   Some Considerations on Terminology

Before moving on, it is of fundamental importance to clarify the terms used in this monograph. Throughout the introduction part, I have used the terms *psychic, paranormal, supernormal and anomalous* interchangeably. But although there are similarities, each of these terms highlight a certain attitude toward the experiences under investigation, reflecting the cultural milieu and scientific disputes surrounding its emergence. The examination of such disputes provides some rich insight into the relationship between parapsychology and religion and will help pave the way for the next parts.

2.1   *Supernormal, Psychic, Parapsychological, and Paranormal*

The term "supernormal" was coined by Myers "on the analogy of abnormal" and based on the idea that these experiences apparently belong to "a more advanced stage of evolution" (Gurney, Myers, and Podmore, 1886, p. XLVI). According to Myers, the supernormal is either a faculty or phenomenon which evidence "laws higher, in a psychical aspect, than are discerned in action in every-day life" (p. XLVI). Despite the apparent similarity, Myer's definition of "supernormal" differs, however, from the old term "supernatural". For him ...

> ... the word *supernatural* is open to grave objections; it assumes that there is something outside nature, and it has become associated with arbitrary interference with law. Now there is no reason to suppose that the psychical phenomena with which we deal are less a part of nature, or less subject to defined and fixed law, than any other phenomena. Some of them appear to indicate a higher evolutionary level than the mass of men have yet attained [...] a transcendental world as fully as in the world of sense.
>
> MYERS, 1903, vol. 1, p. xxii

Thus, for Myers, the supernormal, although entailing the possibility of a transcendental realm, it is not outside nature (I shall return to Myers' ideas in part four). The term is still eventually used by contemporary authors (e.g., Rock, 2014), but much less often than options such as 'psychic', 'anomalous', 'paranormal' or 'psi'. Myers' hypothesis that such phenomena indicate a higher aspect of spiritual evolution is not necessarily endorsed by all parapsychologists (see part four for further discussion). More recently, the term 'supernormal' appeared as part of the title of a popular parapsychology book (Radin, 2013).

Of British origin, the term "psychic" was often used interchangeably with "psychological" during the late-19th and early-20th centuries. It was only after the founding of the SPR that the term began to be associated with telepathy and spiritualist phenomena (Coon, 1992). The term "Parapsychological", in its turn, originated in Germany with Dessoir, but was popularized in the U.S. by Rhine, McDougall, and others with the aim of differentiating their laboratory studies from the non-academic interest in psychic phenomena (Alvarado, 2006). For Rhine (1934, p. 7), the term 'parapsychology' implied that this research area should be placed not "outside psychology" but "beside" it. Instead of 'psychic' or 'psychical', parapsychologists began to use "psi", a more neutral (and non-explanatory) term. Today, variations such as 'psi occurrences' and 'psi-related experiences' are often preferred. However, it is not infrequent to find both 'psychical' and 'psi' (or 'parapsychological') in the literature. The word "paranormal" is virtually synonymous with previous terms (Thalbourne, 2003a) and is widely employed in the psychological literature.

2.2   *Anomalous*

Between the late 1980s and early 1990s, the term 'anomalous' also began to be employed in substitution to (or in complement with) 'paranormal'. A new field, termed *Anomalistic Psychology*, was developed (Reed, 1988; Zusne and Jones, 1989). The roots of this field can be found some time earlier in the work of anthropologist Roger Wescott whom, inspired by the writings of Charles Hoy Fort (1874–1932), coined the term 'anomalistics,' defined as the "serious and systematic study of all phenomena that fail to fit the picture of reality provided for us by common sense or by the established sciences" (Clark, 1993, p. 7). Here, the emphasis resides on the non-ordinariness of such phenomena, rather than on positive, spiritual, or evolutionary aspects as seen in Myers' definition of 'supernormal'. Also, these phenomena are said to "fail to fit the picture of reality" and "common sense". But what should we understand by reality and common sense?

Cardeña, Lynn, and Krippner's (2014, p. 4) definition is clearer in this regard and indicates that the notions of reality and common sense implied by the term anomalous are determined culturally. For them, an anomalous experience is ...

> ... an uncommon experience (e.g., synesthesia), or one that, although experienced by a significant number of persons (e.g., an experience interpreted as telepathic), is believed to markedly deviate from ordinary experience or from the usually accepted explanations of *reality according to Western mainstream science.*
>
> p. 4, italics added

In contrast to 'psychic', 'supernormal' and 'paranormal', the term 'anomalous' has emerged in a context of more skepticism toward claims of psychic phenomena, particularly under the influence of cognitive theories. It also has a wider meaning in comparison to previous terms, entailing a variety of scientifically unexplained phenomena not traditionally investigated by parapsychologists – from reports of alien abductions to alleged encounters with cryptozoological creatures such as the Bigfoot or the Loch Ness Monster. Whereas Rhine placed parapsychology "besides" psychology, the advocates of anomalistic psychology do not necessarily agree with the scientific legitimacy of parapsychological investigations and often prioritize psychological explanations – such as magical thinking and cognitive biases – over unconventional ones. For anomalistic psychologists, paranormal experiences are "weird", strange experiences (Shermer, 2002) for which psychology must provide a rational explanation. In the words of one of its main promoters, Chris French (2001, p. 1), the aim of anomalistic psychology is to ...

> ... explain paranormal and related beliefs and ostensibly paranormal experiences in terms of known (or knowable) psychological and physical factors. It is directed at understanding *bizarre experiences* that many people have, without assuming that there is anything paranormal involved.
> Italics added

Most anomalistic psychologists acknowledge the fact that anomalous experiences are not necessarily pathological, even if they describe them as "weird" or "bizarre". Still, the term 'anomalous' is very often used in reference to psychotic and dissociative experiences in both clinical and nonclinical populations (e.g., Menezes Jr., 2012; Sass et al., 2013). Indeed, researchers investigating psychotic disorders and schizotypy may use 'anomalous' and 'psychotic' interchangeably (e.g., Cicero et al., 2017; Peters et al., 2017). I discuss some of this literature in the next part.

Notwithstanding its skeptical origins, the term 'anomalous' is also of widespread use among parapsychologists. Derivations such as "anomalous cognition" (covering phenomena previously subsumed by the term extra-sensory perception), "anomalous retroactive influences on cognition and affect" (referring to both alleged *precognition* – or "cognitive awareness" of future events – and *premonition* – or "affective apprehension" of such events, Bem, 2011, p. 407), and "anomalous perturbation" (in reference to psychokinesis) are now widely employed in research articles, books, and academic discussions, either by skeptics or those most sympathetic to parapsychology. A series of laboratories and research groups devoted to parapsychological research added the word 'anomalous' to their names, as is the case with the Center for Research on Consciousness and Anomalous Psychology (CERCAP) at Lund University, Sweden, and the Centre for the Study of Anomalous Psychological Processes (CSAPP) at The University of Northampton, UK.

2.3 *Other Variations*

Such instances of terminological appropriation suggest that the new terms developed to account for these experiences were not the result exclusively of attempts to define them but indicated (at least in part) certain strategic maneuvers to avoid the popularization and stigmatization related to previous terms. Thus, instead of 'psychic', Rhine employed 'psi' or 'parapsychological'; instead of 'paranormal' or 'psychic', many authors now use 'anomalous'. Yet, some others prefer to use 'exceptional' (e.g., White, 1997; Evrard, 2013), 'non-ordinary' (Schmidt, 2017; Lynn, 2017) or 'unusual' (Peters et al., 2017).

In the field of transpersonal psychology, the term 'transpersonal' – defined as "people's experiences of temporarily transcending our usual identification with our limited biological, historical, cultural and personal self" (Tart, 2002, p. 39) is preferred and has a broader meaning in comparison to 'psi' and 'psychic' while entailing some of the same experiences. Transpersonal psychologists are interested not only in psi occurrences but also in mystical and contemplative experiences not traditionally studied by parapsychologists (Servadio, 1987). To complicate things further, some psychologists of religion have also acknowledged the profound interconnection between psychic/anomalous and religious experiences (e.g., Oesterreich, 1921, 1930; Thouless, 1971; Hood Jr., 2005; Taves, 2014, 2020).

2.4   *A Sociohistorical Perspective*
Putting aside these terminological subtleties, the fact is that the different terms available (transpersonal, psychic, paranormal, psi, exceptional, anomalous ...) are virtually interchangeable. In most cases, they constituted either attempts to overcome the stigmatization suffered by previous terms or adaptations to a specific research field. From a socio-historical perspective, all these terms share an important characteristic: they are technical, secular definitions of experiences understood, in the past, as belonging almost exclusively to the domain of religious and mystical experience. As I already pointed out elsewhere:

> Partly due to the privatization of religion in Western societies, we began to look at those reports of esoteric phenomena through the lens of the individual; hence the emphasis on 'experiences' rather than on a definite corpus of collective beliefs and dogmas. This was due to a long process of historical transformations, from the search for a more direct relationship with the divine in Pentecostalism and the Charismatic Movement, without the necessary and irrevocable intermediation of a priest, to counterculture and the New Age movement which exhorted a direct experience of the transcendent through a series of practices and psychedelic substances. More recently, psychologists became masters in 'exorcizing' the more metaphysical aspects of these experiences in favor of their neurophysiological, cognitive and personality correlates. The rise of popular attention devoted to practices such as meditation and mindfulness in the last decade (even if without the assumption of mysticism) suggests that this shift from the collective to the individual, from a sacralized to a secular conception of the spiritual, has partly become culturally mainstream.
>
> MARALDI, 2020a, p. 22

From this perspective, the term 'anomalous' is the culmination of a long process of secularization which has created a sort of cultural vacuum; in this context, what is not understood or assimilated becomes 'weird', 'bizarre', 'anomalous':

> It is tempting to explain such terminological transformations as natural or necessary developments of the accumulated knowledge regarding such experiences. The fact is that we can only do so by assuming the superiority of Western culture to the detriment of other cultural contexts. We need to realize that as we study these issues, we also help to create part of what we observe ... [This terminological debate] reveals both our ignorance about the nature of these experiences and the current lack of a broader worldview to integrate them.
>
> MARALDI ET AL., 2018, p. 63

In other societies, including indigenous communities, these experiences would be categorized or interpreted in very different ways, and would not necessarily be 'anomalous' or 'unusual' in relation to cultural norms, practices, and worldviews (McClenon, 2002). There are many ways through which "societies and groups shape or constrain identity, self-perception, and the report of anomalous experiences" (Maraldi and Krippner, 2019, p. 307). Hence, we must be aware of the assumptions implicit in our terminological choices, especially when such terms as "weird" or "bizarre" are employed.

Given the impossibility of currently resolving all the complex terminological issues hitherto presented, I leave behind the search for the ideal term. In subsequent parts, I will give preference to the terms 'psychic', 'psi', and 'paranormal' for three main reasons: 1) the term 'psychic' is found both in contemporary studies and in the old psychical literature, 2) the general term 'psi' is of widespread use in current parapsychological research, and 3) the term 'paranormal' is often used by contemporary psychologists (see next part). However, these terms might be supplemented by others throughout the text when the work of other authors is cited or discussed.

2.5   *Experiences and Events*

Thus far, I have been employing the words *occurrence* (or *event*) and *experience* without clearly differentiating the two, what can lead to some confusion. In many cases, reports of psychic abilities or events are limited to personal testimony and do not accompany any objective evidence of their legitimacy. But there are other cases where striking similarities between the content of a psychic experience and an objective event can be verified, suggesting that the experience apparently conveys veridical information.

An illustrative and historical example is the vision reported by the mystic Emanuel Swendenborg towards the end of the year 1759. At the occasion, he was visiting the house of a resident merchant in Gothenburg when he suddenly had the vision of a fire taking place in Stockholm. According to Kant (1766, p. 95), the report from Stockholm, which arrived two days later, "agreed entirely, it is said, with Swedenborg's visions". Here, it is precisely the agreement between *experience* and *event* that makes Swedenborg's testimony of particular interest to parapsychology. Although the psychological and social processes that help shape such experiences are certainly important, parapsychologists are mostly concerned with the extent to which experience and event coincide and whether conventional explanations (such as a chance occurrence) can account for it.

Krippner and Schroll (2014) provide us with useful criteria to differentiate between experiences and events. According to the authors, an "event refers to physical factors, or the impingement of sensory data on our neural receptors". On the other hand, an experience "is the internalization of the event, and is shaped or interpreted through our particular cultural belief systems" (p. 6). Krippner and Schroll also differentiate between authenticity and veracity with *authenticity* being the honesty with which a person describers his/her experience (instead of lying or fraudulently producing a false event) and *veracity* being the correspondence between an experiential report and an event. An experiential report may be authentic – in the sense that the person is honestly and accurately describing his/her experience and/or interpretations of it – but not veridical – in the sense that it does not correspond with the event. It may turn out, for example, that a clairvoyant's description of a distant place is incompatible with the objective features of that place, even though he/she is not lying.

The differentiation between experiences and events bears some important philosophical implications. An idealist or relativist can always question the very existence of a real world outside our minds or the possibility of finding the "truth" behind the experience. The issue of what is reality or whether it exists is far beyond the more limited purposes of this work. On the other hand, parapsychology presupposes an objective reality, since it is based on the conviction that claims of psychic phenomena can be scientifically demonstrated or refuted. This can only be done if there is an Archimedean point (in our case, the scientific method) from which an observer can objectively examine the subject of inquiry. Thus, it seems appropriate here to differentiate between experiences and events, even though this differentiation may be tenuous or questionable for some. I will give preference in the following pages to the term 'experience', but will also use 'event', 'occurrence' or 'phenomenon' whenever I want to emphasize the possibility of real psychic processes underlying reports of psychic experiences. In my view, these terms do not represent different things, but different aspects of the same thing. Experience and event are just different ways to look at the same processes, as suggested by Krippner and Schroll (2014). The question of whether the event (or events) underlying an experience is (are) indeed paranormal is irrelevant to our distinction.

The struggle to differentiate between experience and event has a long history in psychology and can be traced back to the separation between psychical research and psychology of religion at the turn of the 20th century. Taves (2014) has argued that the preference for *experiences* over *phenomena* resulted from attempts to differentiate psychology from psychical research, comprising another instance of the *boundary-work* described by Sommer (2012) and others. According to Taves (2014, p. 377):

> Those most passionately interested in psychical research insisted on maintaining "extraordinary phenomena", for which they sought objective evidence, as their object of study, whereas those interested in studying religion were willing to shift their focus to "extraordinary experiences" and derive their evidence from subjective reports.

In this and the next parts, I will argue that a clear differentiation between psychic and religious beliefs and experiences is often difficult to make. There are all sorts of gradation between the two, even though some authors have preferred to categorize them separately. This problem was acknowledged by the founding fathers of psychology but was subsequently obscured by the boundary-work carried out to separate psychology from psychical research. The pioneers of these two fields could "ascribe very different meanings to experiences that were very similar in terms of their underlying phenomenology" (Taves, 2014, p. 394), a state of affairs that might have hindered the establishment of a reciprocal and productive dialogue. Taves (2014) suggests that such differences could be overcome with the "open up [of] an interdisciplinary space" (p. 394) where collaborative discussions about terminological issues and the development of comparative studies and analyses would take place. This monograph aims precisely to initiate such an interdisciplinary conversation.

2.6   *Belief*

In this direction, it is essential to bring to the discussion another fundamental term: belief. The notion of belief is embedded in Krippner and Schroll's definition of experience: "... the internalization of the event [...] is shaped or interpreted through our particular cultural *belief* systems" [italics added]

(2014, p. 6). The authors seem to imply that there is no clear boundary between an experience and its interpretation, since the experience will always be construed, to a lesser or greater extent, based on particular beliefs and expectations. Also, there is no clear difference here between belief and interpretation. However, if we take a closer look, it becomes clear that the two are not identical. A belief is "the acceptance of the truth, reality, or validity of something (e.g., a phenomenon, a person's veracity), particularly in the absence of substantiation" (American Psychological Association, 2015, p. 119). According to this definition, a belief presupposes commitment to a certain interpretation of a phenomenon. In contrast, this is not required of all interpretations. One might raise an interpretation for the sake of explanation, in the manner of a guess or conjecture, without necessarily accepting it as 'the truth'. In this sense, beliefs are interpretations but not all interpretations are beliefs. It is one thing to consider telepathy as a possible interpretation for certain experiences, and quite another to believe in the reality of telepathy; the difference here is the same for "entertaining" versus "endorsing" (Schooler et al., 2018). Despite sometimes resisting all counterarguments, beliefs are not completely immune to change or refutation (et al., Shariff et al., 2008).

The APA dictionary describes beliefs as lacking "substantiation", but the degree to which a belief is not substantiated by evidence may vary considerably from one case to another. Science is also based on beliefs, but it is quite unusual in everyday life to speak of scientific beliefs; it is more common to speak of hypotheses and theories (which are, in fact, elaborated systems of belief submitted to systematic investigation). Latour (2005) challenges the distinction according to which religion should be described in terms of belief and science in terms of knowledge. For him, science also requires a good dose of faith, and religion is more than mere belief. In the notion of belief, the complexity and diversity of the manifestations of religion are reduced to their cognitive components, such as statements about the veracity of a phenomenon or allegation. When we consider the variety of religious expressions in rituals, symbols, practices, and experiences across different cultures, it becomes clear that religion is more than belief.

A similar argument could be extended to paranormal experiences: they may sometimes be reported in the apparent absence of previous belief or, on the contrary, be seldom reported by assumed believers (McClenon, 2002; Irwin et al., 2013a; Dein, 2016). Despite their profound interrelationship, paranormal beliefs and experiences may evidence different prevalence rates and psychological correlates (Evrard, 2013). Hence, paranormality is more than belief.

Evrard (2013) observes that the psychological literature on paranormal *beliefs* is more abundant when compared with the literature concerning paranormal *experiences*. As I shall argue in the next part, the preference by contemporary psychologists for the term 'belief' is in part explained by their negative attitude toward religious and paranormal allegations. For many psychologists, such allegations necessarily lack "substantiation"; in other words, they are *irrational*. Therefore, they are not descriptions of verifiable occurrences, but wrong, confused interpretations of psychological, biological, and physical events. Although I often use the word 'belief' in this monograph, I must draw attention to the fact that 'belief' is more an ideological than a scientific concept. In the context of the psychology of the paranormal, "this ideology is manifested in the urge to explain away or provide a rational account of the supposedly irrational beliefs of others" (Bowie, 2014, p. 20).

2.7   *Religion and the Paranormal*

At the end of the 20th century, a debate took place in the psychological literature concerning the definition of the paranormal. The 'classic' definition espoused by parapsychologists refer to those phenomena most frequently investigated from an experimental, laboratory approach: the so-called extrasensory perception (or ESP, which includes telepathy, precognition and clairvoyance), and psychokinesis (or PK). Cardeña (2018, p. 664) observes, however, that the term anomalous cognition is preferred to ESP: "ESP is a misleading term because it suggests perception as the mediating mechanism, although few if any psi researchers nowadays assume this to be the case". Given its widespread use, I will eventually employ the term ESP throughout the monograph, particularly when citing the work of other authors, although giving preference to psi.

Besides ESP or anomalous cognition, parapsychologists often include in their list phenomena such as distant healing intention (covering practices such as reiki and intercessory prayer), out-of-body experiences, near-death experiences, channeling / mediumship, and past-life experiences (usually cases of adults and children who claim to remember previous lives). However, the participation of non-parapsychologists in research on paranormal beliefs – such as psychologists and sociologists – have been responsible for a significant extension of the definition of the paranormal. According to these researchers, the 'paranormal' is not restricted to phenomena usually studied by parapsychologists but includes all major forms of religious and supernatural beliefs (Irwin, 2004). The main argument in favor of this conceptual expansion is that at least some of the cognitive and psychosocial factors underlying the endorsement of religious and paranormal beliefs are the same (Goode, 2000; Irwin, 2004; Northcote, 2007; Baker et al., 2016).

In fact, both religious adherents and non-religious people may believe in the existence of life after death, the efficacy of spiritual healing and the ability of some individuals to predict the occurrence of events that could not have been foreseen, although the interpretation given to these allegations may vary according to a religious or non-religious perspective (Flannely et al., 2006; Goode, 2000). In the Bible, for example, there are numerous accounts of seemingly paranormal occurrences, such as premonitory dreams, prophetic visions, and anomalous cures (Sparks, 2001). Indeed, some studies have found that religious adherents and theists tend to hold paranormal beliefs more often than those who do not belong to a religion or are non-theists (Orenstein, 2002; Rice, 2003. Thalbourne, 2003b). In the same vein, paranormal believers are more likely than disbelievers to describe themselves as religious, to say that religion and prayer is important to them, to read books or articles about religion, and to attend religious meetings (Thalbourne and Houtkooper, 2002). Hergovitch et al. (2005) obtained significant correlations between a measure of paranormal belief and various indices of religiosity including intrinsic religiosity. Some authors have also suggested that both paranormal and religious beliefs are efficacious in reducing death anxiety (Persinger and Makarec, 1990; Tobacyk, 1983a), thereby indicating a common ground in terms of basic psychodynamic mechanisms. In a review of the relevant literature, Lindeman and Svedholm (2012) argued that beliefs variously termed as paranormal, religious, magical or superstitious share some of the same basic cognitive characteristics, and suggested researchers in these different areas to integrate current lines of research.

On the other hand, several other authors have defended that there are fundamental incompatibilities between paranormal and religious beliefs. Emmons and Sobal (1981), Stark and Bainbridge (1986) and Persinger and Makarec (1990) argued that paranormal beliefs might serve as substitutes for religious beliefs. They claim that the void left by the decline of traditional religious institutions in Western societies, which used to guide cultural values and beliefs, may have been partially filled by alternative spiritual practices and groups. Sparks (2001) remind us that many paranormal beliefs and practices are not endorsed by religious adherents, especially those that contradict established dogmas – such as reincarnation and cartomancy, which are condemned by Catholicism (see also Haynes, 1964). Sparks also points out that religious beliefs are not subject to empirical evaluation. Hence, their endorsement is much more a matter of faith, while certain paranormal claims are amenable to experimental investigation – such as precognition and psychokinesis.

However, for many religious believers and theologians, there is no obvious difference between paranormal and religious experiences; for some, parapsychological research is seen as relevant to an understanding "of all of the great issues of religion" (Grace, 1970, p. 9) and "closely linked with the history and theology of religious belief" (Haynes, 1964, p. 289) – see also Thurston (1933). Haynes (1964) observes, for example, that some of the earliest representants of Catholic Church theorized about paranormal phenomena such as pre-monitions, anomalous cures, and levitation, among them Thomas Aquinas (1225–1274) and Pope Benedict XIV (1675–1758). The investigation of paranormal claims comprised an important part of many canonization processes and the rigor with which the evidence for such phenomena was analyzed sometimes paralleled those of modern parapsychological and psychological studies (Thurston, 1952; Haynes, 1964).

Baker et al. (2016) suggested that paranormal and religious beliefs show significant psychological, physiological and ontological similarities, thereby evidencing an underlying common core. However, organized religions tend to focus on a specific set of beliefs, practices, and experiences, banishing other notions which are incongruent with the established interpretive framework. According to the authors, this explains why individuals not particularly tied to a religion tend to score higher on measures of paranormal belief and experience – see also Laubach (2004). For Baker et al. (2016, p. 337), the distinctions between paranormal and religious beliefs and experiences comprise "cultural boundaries [...] created and sustained by interpretive communities".

Overall, there is little doubt that the definitions for paranormal and religious beliefs overlap considerably in the psychological and parapsychological literatures, even though some authors have suggested differentiating the two (e.g., Williams et al., 2009). A clear-cut distinction between traditional religious beliefs and paranormal concepts may be difficult to establish, as beliefs in life after death, premonition, and spiritual healing suggest (McClenon, 2002; Baker et al., 2016).

This terminological impasse is due, in part, to the lack of a consensual, widely accepted definition of religion, which is a long-standing problem in the fields of Religious Studies and Psychology of Religion. If we bring to the debate terms such as 'secular religion', 'implicit religion' and other similar notions, this might complicate further the differentiation between religious and paranormal concepts or practices. Furthermore, the correlation between paranormal beliefs and religiosity may differ according to how religiosity is measured. For example, Thalbourne and O'Brien (1999) found that paranormal belief was positively correlated with a general measure of religiosity but had no significant correlation with variables such as religious puritanism and frequency of Bible reading.

Although some have criticized the terminological expansion established for the definition of paranormal belief, there is agreement on the fact that the relationship between traditional religious ideas and contemporary paranormal concepts remains a fruitful area for investigation (Tobacyk, 2004; Goode, 2000; Irwin, 2004; Baker et al., 2016). In this direction, some authors have found that the relationship between paranormal and religious beliefs is curvilinear, with paranormal beliefs increasing alongside religious beliefs, but then decreasing when religious beliefs become particularly strong (Baker et al., 2010; Bader et al., 2012). For example, a strong commitment to traditional Protestant religious beliefs was shown to be negatively related to paranormal beliefs (Hillstrom and Strachan, 2000). Hergovitch et al. (2005) identified a positive association between paranormal belief and religiosity for a sample of Austrians. Nonetheless, the association was stronger among individuals without affiliation compared to Catholics and Protestants. These findings are in accordance with both the delimitation proposed by some authors between traditional religious beliefs and more contemporary, alternative spiritualities (Farias and Lalljee, 2008), as well as with the "bounded affinity" (Baker et al., 2016) between paranormal and religious beliefs defended by others.

A third model suggests that religiosity is a particular expression of spirituality, often characterized by conservatism and traditionalism (Hood et al., 2018); according to this view, spirituality serves as a bridge between religion and the paranormal. However, when the content of paranormal experiences conflict in some way with religious doctrine, these experiences tend to be less valued and reported and may even be completely rejected. This is congruent with research showing that "when samples are carefully selected for their religious identification, paranormal experiences are infrequently cited (if at all) as instances of religious experiences" (Hood et al., 2018, p. 371).

2.8   *Spirituality*

Despite the widespread popularity and scholarly attention received by the concept of 'spirituality' in recent decades, there is much debate about how to define it. I have presented and discussed the conceptual controversy regarding spirituality in more detail elsewhere (Maraldi, 2020a). For the purposes of this work, I define spirituality, based on Huguelet and Koenig (2007), as "a general and relatively informal adherence to transcendent meanings and beliefs that may or may not arise from involvement with a religious community or belief system" (Maraldi, 2020a, p. 772).

The relationship between religiosity and spirituality is complex and still unresolved. Some authors suggest that spirituality may or may not include a religious dimension, while others affirm that spirituality is a contemporary, individual alternative to religion. Marshall and Olson (2018) argue that spirituality is neither religious nor irreligious, but a step on the path between religion and non-religion.

Research on spirituality has important connections with the investigation of paranormal beliefs and experiences. Words such as 'spirituality' and 'spiritual' are often employed by paranormal believers to refer to their world-views and beliefs (Thalbourne and Houtkooper, 2002; Maraldi and Farias, 2019). Accordingly, many factorial studies have found that paranormal beliefs and experiences are basic components of spirituality (MacDonald, 2000, 2015; Schofield et al., 2016). Paranormal beliefs are also better predictors of scores on measures of spirituality when compared with variables such as subjective well-being and purpose in life (Lindeman et al., 2012). More importantly, many parapsychologists have explicitly stated that their research bear implications for the definition and understanding of spirituality (e.g., Tart, 2002; Walach et al., 2009; Baruš and Mossbridge, 2017).

The interconnections between the study of psychic/paranormal experience and the field of spirituality are so many that one might question whether it would be more appropriate in this monograph to speak of spirituality rather than religion or religiosity. But it should be remarked that a similar debate also permeates the field of psychology of religion. The division 36 of the American Psychological Association is currently named *Society for the Psychology of Religion and Spirituality*, and this after many years being named 'Psychology of Religion' (Reuder, 1999; Hood, 2012). Several handbooks in the field now include the broader title of psychology of religion *and spirituality* (or only spirituality), such as the *Handbook for the Psychology of Religion and Spirituality* (Paloutzian and Park, 2013), the *APA Handbook of Psychology, Religion, and Spirituality* (Pargament, 2013) and *The Oxford Handbook of Psychology and Spirituality* (Miller, 2013). Still, some authors and organizations resist a terminological expansion. Of European origin, the *International Association for the Psychology of Religion* does not include spirituality in its name, even though the subject of spirituality is frequently addressed in its biannual events. Aletti et al. (2019) has recently argued in favor of 'psychology of religion' (without spirituality), noting the broad, unspecific character of the notion of spirituality.

For my part, I see spirituality and religiosity as profoundly interconnected concepts, even sometimes as indistinguishable. Spirituality probably tells us more about certain transformations and expressions of contemporary religiosity, particularly in Western societies, than it points to a different, clearly identifiable phenomenon (Maraldi, 2020a). This brings us to James' (1902/2002, p. 29–30) definition of religion as "the feelings, acts and experiences of individual men in their solitude, so far as they apprehend themselves to stand in relation to whatever they may consider the divine". This seems more like a description of what we would call today as spirituality (Hood, 2012).

The history of spirituality crosses the history of parapsychology in important ways, since the same secularization processes that allowed the critique of organized religion also seemed to have allowed the emergence and proliferation of a more individualized and experience-oriented religiosity that refuses to just reiterate religious tradition but requires an experimental demonstration of its tenets and a direct experience of the sacred. From this perspective, if we want to understand the implications of parapsychological findings for the psychology of religion in the contemporary scene, we should take spirituality into consideration.

2.9   *Mystical Experience*

Streib et al. (2020) define spirituality as an "individualized-experience-oriented" religiosity. In support of their definition, they found that more spiritual than religious people associate 'spirituality' with mystical experiences of all-connectedness, as well as score higher on the Mysticism scale (Hood, 1975). In a related vein, some authors have equated mystical and paranormal experiences (e.g., Hall, 1909; Thurston, 1952; Greeley, 1975; Hardy, 1979). Wulff (2014), for instance, describes the mystical experience as a subcategory of paranormal/anomalous experience. Hood et al. (2018) also observe that measures of mystical and paranormal experiences are often positively correlated and usually form a single factor, indicating that these two types of experience are "connected in the popular mind" (p. 370).

Servadio (1985) largely concurs with the view that the lives of Eastern or Western mystics from Saint Joseph of Copertino (1603–1663) to Ramakrishna (1836–1886) provide parapsychologists with many examples of possible paranormal phenomena including reports of levitation, spiritual healing, clairvoyance, telepathy, and various other allegations. He mentions a series of potential research paradigms with which parapsychologists can investigate claims of psychic phenomena reputed to mystics. However, Servadio also acknowledges that "the duality which forms the core both of our daily empirical experience and also of the subject-object distinction, which is essential to scientific observation, is transcended in mystical experience" (p. 9). The ineffability of some mystical accounts also makes them less suitable for parapsychological experimentation. Finally, mystics may attribute little importance to such phenomena, privileging their moral or philosophical implications instead. Indeed, some spiritual traditions clearly differentiate psychic abilities from other aspects of spiritual life. In Patanjali's *Yoga sutras*, for instance, psychic phenomena (or *Siddhis*) are depicted as distractions from further spiritual development (Braud, 2008). It seems thus that a closer look at the teachings of mystics and their traditions may reveal important differences between mystical and paranormal experiences. As Hood et al. (2018, p. 371) observe: "It is unlikely that members of the general population make such distinctions, because they usually lack either the experiential base or the conceptual sophistication to make such distinctions".

I argue that although research on parapsychological and mystical experiences do not fully overlap, there is nevertheless a common ground between the mystical and the paranormal. Mystical traditions have anticipated ideas now taken for granted by some parapsychologists, such as the notions that consciousness is fundamental to all reality and all things are interconnected at a fundamental level (Radin, 2006; Walach et al., 2009). If the early psychical research was chiefly influenced by the spiritualist movement, the parapsychology developed from the 1960's onwards found much inspiration in the philosophies and contemplative practices of Eastern mysticism, following a trend also observed among transpersonal psychologists. This change of reference frame also accompanied a growing interest in altered states of consciousness including those elicited by meditation (Asprem, 2010; Kripal, 2012; Cardeña, 2019). A more peripheric literature also explored the many relations of parapsychology with Christian and Jewish traditions (e.g., Thurston, 1953; Wright, 1955; Bazak, 1972; Nicol, 1976). Based on this substantial array of analogies and approximations, it seems that parapsychology and the scientific study of mysticism have much to gain from an interdisciplinary dialogue. I shall explore further some of these interconnections in part four.

3   The Psychology of the Paranormal: A Critique

A significant part of the work carried out by the pioneers of modern psychology consisted in analyzing and contesting certain popular beliefs (from astrology to spiritualism), based on the then-recent contributions of research on behavior, memory, perception, and other basic psychological processes. An Illustrative example can be found in the writings of psychologist Joseph Jastrow (1900). For him, the critical examination of claims of psychic phenomena was part of a larger program to disseminate the knowledge produced by experimental psychologists to the public at large and, in doing so, help establish the newly founded discipline of psychology. Jastrow (1930/1960, p. 150) was convinced that the "popularization of psychology was essential to its public appreciation and official support". Because the lay public manifested much interest in psychic phenomena (Coons, 1992), this topic became one of Jastrow's preferred targets. Such "anomalous mental phenomena", in Jastrow's own words (Jastrow, 1900, p. vi), are "problems upon which psychology has an authoritative charge to make to the public jury" (p. viii). But in contrast to

James, Flournoy or Jung, Jastrow did not believe that such matters were central to the understanding of the mind. He deeply regretted "that the dispossession of fable requires more resolute and more elaborate exposition than the unfoldment of fact" (p. ix). For him, psychic phenomena are illusions which psychology should confront and destroy; only the psychological principles derived from their analysis should remain. His approach would inspire a series of other skeptical works (e.g., Rawcliffe, 1959; Shermer, 2002).

Jastrow was one of the heirs of a long philosophical tradition going back to the Enlightenment period. Inspired by the critical perspective toward the supernatural endorsed by philosophers such as David Hume (1711–1776) and Voltaire (1694–1778), Jastrow and other founding fathers of psychology believed to be their duty to explain and combat religious and psychical beliefs about the mind. Influenced by the dream of a future without religion – considered as the main representant of irrationality and obscurantism – authors such as Freud (1907/1924) and Leuba (1916) predicted that one day beliefs such as God and immortality would disappear, eclipsed by the gradual development of science. Despite his deep interest in telepathy (Evrard et al., 2017), Freud nevertheless expressed his concern that psychoanalysis could become associated with occultism, a remnant of "obsolete convictions" which should be studied with the sole purpose of eliminating it "once and for all [...] from the realm of material reality" (Freud, 1922/1953b, p. 57–58).

The decades went by and Freud and Leuba's prediction has almost completely failed. While the endorsement of traditional religious beliefs decreased in some countries, especially in Western Europe, it remained strong in contexts such as Latin America, Asia, and the United States (Casanova, 2007; Martín, 2017). Religiosity became less easily captured in terms of denominational affiliation and church attendance but continued to be relevant and influential in the individual and collective levels (Greeley, 1995). In its turn, spirituality is on the rise (Loewenthal, 2018) and the prevalence of paranormal beliefs and reports of paranormal experiences is high in different countries (e.g., Greeley, 1975; Palmer, 1979; McClenon, 1988; Haraldsson and Houtkooper, 1991; Castro, Burrows, and Wooffitt, 2014; Maraldi and Krippner, 2019; Maraldi and Farias, 2020). Some findings also suggest, as opposed to the classic theory of secularization, that people from wealthy and highly secularized countries are more suspicious of scientific and technological development, perhaps because they are more aware of both its potentialities and limitations (Zuckerman et al., 2016).

3.1   *Cognitive Biases and Paranormal Belief*
However, in contrast to this complex and diversified scenario, contemporary psychological research on paranormal beliefs still relies on the same arguments

and perspectives espoused by Jastrow and other critics of Victorian spiritualism and psychical research, actualizing the Enlightenment heritage based on more recent findings. When, from the 1960s onwards, the interest in paranormal phenomena, psychedelics and Eastern mysticism increased (Hanegraff, 1996), many psychologists emerged to argue – reportedly in defense of science – that belief in the paranormal should be discouraged and extinguished. In an evident violation of Flournoy's principles of Hamlet and Laplace, which invite us to act with moderation and avoid one-sized perspectives, the proponents of what Irwin (2004) has called the "cognitive deficit hypothesis" state that those who believe in paranormal phenomena are gullible and have little intelligence, being therefore susceptible to endorse "demonstrably absurd" beliefs (Singer and Benassi, 1981, p. 49) against which they would be unable to counterargue (Alcock, 1981; Kurtz, 1996; Randi, 1992). In this context, paranormal beliefs and experiences are regarded "as cognitive aberrations within established frameworks of problem-solving or decision making" (Lange et al., 2019, p. 347) and believers are often characterized "as being cognitively inferior to disbelievers" (Roe, 1999, p. 85). For Singer and Benassi (1981), paranormal beliefs are "pathologies of reasoning" (p. 49). For Paul Kurtz (1996, p. 493), the paranormal and religion are "two sources of unreason in democratic society".

The pejorative terms employed by proponents of the cognitive deficit hypothesis make clear an underlying prejudice against their object of study: "fallacious beliefs" (Leonard, 2014), "weird beliefs" (Boudry et al., 2015), "ontological confusions" (Lindeman et al., 2015), "pseudo-profound bullshit" (Pennycook et al., 2015), "illusory beliefs" (Donizzetti and Petrillo, 2017), "irrational beliefs" (Žeželj and Lazarević, 2019), among many others. Given that most such beliefs are endorsed by members of religious or spiritual groups and are widespread in certain cultures, the above-mentioned terms could eventually be construed as instances of religious and cultural discrimination. Some other terms such as "beliefs in unsubstantiated claims" (Bensley et al., 2018) and "epistemically suspect beliefs" (Majima et al., 2020) are less pejorative but convey basically the same meaning, that is, that paranormal beliefs are irrational and most likely false.

But what the empirical evidence has to say about the cognitive deficit hypothesis? Researchers devised different ways to test it ranging from self-report measures and performance-based tasks to experimental and neurophysiological paradigms. In what follows, I review the main findings from the principal branches of investigation in this area and outline their methodological and conceptual limitations. Additionally, I discuss how research on spirituality and religion may shed light on the underpinnings of paranormal beliefs and propose some methodological recommendations for future research.

3.2   *Intelligence and Critical Thinking*

Many studies found a negative relationship between paranormal beliefs and scores on measures of intelligence, cognitive ability, and critical thinking, thus obtaining support for the cognitive deficit hypothesis (Wierzbicki, 1985; Alcock and Otis, 1980; Roig et al., 1998; Watt and Wiseman, 2002; Lawrence and Peters, 2004; Čavojová et al., 2020). Notwithstanding, Jones et al. (1977) found precisely the opposite pattern, that is, a positive and significant correlation between intelligence and paranormal beliefs. In their turn, Irwin (1991), Korpan et al. (1997), Roe (1999), Royalty (1995) and Thalbourne and Nofi (1997) did not find evidence of a significant correlation between paranormal belief or experience and measures of intelligence, reasoning skills or critical thinking.

Tam and Shia (2004) found a negative correlation with cognitive complexity for traditional religiosity but not for paranormal beliefs. Hergovitch and Arendasy (2005) also did not obtain a significant statistical correlation between critical thinking and paranormal belief and experience, but respondents with low reasoning ability scored slightly higher on traditional religious belief and New Age philosophy. No correlation was found between reasoning ability and reports of paranormal experiences.

As summarized by French and Stone (2014, p. 116): "the evidence is decidedly mixed for lower levels of reasoning ability in general, or critical thinking in particular, in believers compared to non-believers". In some studies, such as that of Wierzbicki (1985), the correlation coefficients were weak in strength and varied according to the task under consideration. Wiseman and Watt (2006) also note the "rather confused pattern of findings" and remark that ...

> ... drawing any strong conclusions from this body of work is problematic, in part, because many of the studies have employed rather general measures (e.g. participants' IQ scores or SAT [scholastic aptitude test] results) that do not directly test the hypothesis that believers are less able than disbelievers to evaluate evidence of alleged psychic ability.

3.3   *Probability Misjudgment and Patternicity*

In terms of probabilistic reasoning (i.e., the ability to estimate how much an event is likely to happen), various studies suggest that paranormal believers tend to underestimate the role of probability in different circumstances (e.g., Blackmore and Troscianko, 1985; Brugger et al., 1990, 1991, 1994). These investigations are particularly relevant to the cognitive deficit hypothesis because many critics have argued that paranormal believers often neglect the likelihood of an event to happen by chance and tend to explain coincidences (e.g., a person dreams with an event that later becomes true) in terms of paranormal phenomena (e.g., premonitory dream). However, Blackmore (1997) found no significant difference between paranormal believers (59%) and non-believers in a sample of 6238 Britons. Musch and Ehrenberg (2002) verified a positive correlation between paranormal belief and probability misjudgment, which disappeared, however, when a measure of academic performance was controlled for. Dagnall et al. (2007) submitted believers and disbelievers to different reasoning tasks and concluded that there was no evidence to suggest that paranormal belief is associated with a general weakness in probabilistic reasoning.

In a review of the evidence bearing on the cognitive deficit hypothesis, Wiseman and Watt (2006, p. 328–329) raised concerns over the methodological adequacy of studies on probability misjudgment, drawing attention to the need of improving ecological validity:

> The probabilistic judgment tasks that have tended to show a significant relationship with belief in psychic ability appear somewhat artificial (e.g. assessing the likelihood of a die producing a certain sequence of numbers), whereas more ecologically valid tasks (e.g. assessing the probability of the type of statements made by a psychic being accurate) have failed to replicate these effects.

Some authors suggested that instead of ignoring the role of probability and chance in everyday circumstances, believers would be more likely than non-believers to attribute patterns to randomness (e.g., recognizing the face of a deceased person in a fuzzy image). Shermer (2011) named this psychological characteristic "patternicity". In support of this notion, Dagnall et al. (2007) found that the tendency to find patterns in randomness significantly predicted paranormal belief. Gianotti et al. (2001) observed that paranormal believers yielded more original results than non-believers in a task of word association when exposed to non-semantically correlated stimuli. The authors explained these findings in terms of both positive (verbal creativity) and negative characteristics (suggestibility to unfounded inferences and a looser criterion of response to semantic noise). Similarly, Riekki et al. (2013) encountered that paranormal and religious believers performed better than skeptics and non-believers at identifying predefined patterns in a face-detection task but were also more prone to illusory face perception.

Other studies found that paranormal believers made more mistakes in a visual identification task despite believing that they had been successful (Blackmore and Moore, 1994) and evidenced more causal illusions (i.e., illusory causal connections between events that are actually unrelated), although this was observed only for ambiguous stimuli and did not affect the ability to identify factual causal relationships (Blanco et al., 2015).

Notwithstanding, in an experimental study, van Elk (2015) found, unexpectedly, that skeptics compared to paranormal believers more often incorrectly classified an ambiguous stimulus as representing a house. In contrast, believers performed at chance level. Also, when believers were asked to categorize a stimulus as representing an agent or a non-agent, no bias toward agency detection was observed. This suggests that believers do not necessarily attribute purpose or agency when they are presented with ambiguous stimuli. Van Elk's experiment also indicates that perceptual biases are not exclusive of paranormal believers.

3.4   *Educational Level*

A series of other studies investigated the role of science education in reducing or discouraging the endorsement of paranormal beliefs. This research is considered important to the cognitive deficit hypothesis because it assumes that fostering scientific reasoning can contribute to discouraging belief in the paranormal. In his studies, Miller (1987) found a strong negative correlation between paranormal belief and scientific education. He observed that the lower the educational level of respondents, the greater the likelihood of endorsing paranormal beliefs. In support of Miller's findings, some investigators indeed verified that university students reported less paranormal beliefs when compared with high school students (Aarnio and Lindeman, 2005; Fitzpatrick and Shook, 1994; Peltzer, 2003; Tobacyk, Miller and Jones, 1984).

In contrast, Broch (2000) and Boy and Michelat (1986) observed that public opinion polls in France indicated a positive correlation between paranormal belief and educational level. In their turn, Farha and Steward (2006) evaluated the responses of 439 university students from the U.S. and concluded that length of university education was related to higher belief in the paranormal – see also Askevis-Leherpeux (1990) for research in France and other countries. Haraldsson (1985) and Haraldsson and Houtkooper (1991) found that, depending on the country, paranormal beliefs and experiences may relate either positively or negatively with educational level. They also verified that, in some cultures, there was no discernible relationship.

Finally, some authors observed that educational level varies depending on the category of belief. For example, belief in extra-sensory perception was higher among better-educated people while traditional religious beliefs such as heaven and hell were negatively affected by education (Wuthnow 1978; Fox 1992; Goode 2000). In a study about the encouragement of beliefs in children, parents who scored higher on paranormal and New Age beliefs were not less encouraging of scientific education, but traditional religious beliefs were associated with weaker encouragement of scientific reasoning (Braswell et al., 2011).

In short, the findings are mixed but suggest that the general education received at the university level may not be sufficient to decrease or suppress belief in the paranormal. An important limitation of such studies is that they do not clearly differentiate the roles of knowledge acquisition and social influence. Do some students abandon their beliefs because they learn how to differentiate science from pseudoscience or because they are socially influenced to do so? It would be important to investigate further whether students are really understanding the workings of science or just responding to social expectations concerning the most appropriate attitude of an academic. Moreover, 'length of university education' is a very generic measure because different factors in university life could have influenced a student's decision to change his/her beliefs beyond developing a more elaborate understanding of the scientific method.

The evidence suggests that courses specifically targeted to debunk (Tobacyk, 1983b; Wesp and Montgomery, 1998) paranormal beliefs are more successful than just providing general science education content (see also Mill et al., 1994). But the ostensible use of educational techniques for the purposes of attacking (or otherwise disseminating) religious and paranormal beliefs raises important ethical concerns, especially in the context of secular states. Such courses are inherently biased and may not do justice to alternative perspectives which are of fundamental importance to the development of critical thinking.

A note should also be made concerning the negative correlation found by some studies between educational level and traditional religious beliefs such as creationism, heaven and hell, and the existence and influence of the devil. By its own nature, survey findings reflect the most popular and predominant perspective about a topic, often neglecting the differences and subtleties that may exist between religious respondents. Theological concepts, for example, may not conform to the same pattern of results. A similar observation can be made regarding paranormal believers, as they might differ in their knowledge of the parapsychological evidence and the philosophical issues underlying the scientific debate on paranormal phenomena (Irwin, 2004).

3.5   *Thinking Styles*

Another area of particular importance to the present discussion concerns the role of intuitive thinking as opposed to analytical thinking in the formation of paranormal beliefs (e.g., Irwin and Young, 2002; Aarnio and Lindeman, 2005; Pennycook et al., 2012; Irwin and Wilson, 2013). While the former is unconscious, fast, automatic, intuitive, and holistic, the latter is described as analytical, conscious, deliberative, and more time-consuming. Considerable research in recent decades has been dedicated to this dual-process model of cognition (e.g., Epstein, 1994; Kahneman, 2003; Evans and Frankish, 2009). Extending the findings of these studies to the investigation of paranormal beliefs, Pennycook et al. (2012, p. 337) have argued that "to the extent that paranormal beliefs are, like religious beliefs, vulnerable to rational and empirical disconfirmation, their rejection should be related to a more analytic cognitive style". In support of their argument, they found that participants with an analytic cognitive style were less likely to endorse paranormal beliefs and to engage in religious activities. However, Pennycook et al. did not evaluate the specific role of intuitive thinking. Other studies have done so and identified a positive association between paranormal belief and an intuitive thinking style (e.g., Aarnio and Lindeman, 2005; Genovese, 2005; Marks et al., 2008).

Nonetheless, in a study by Wolfradt et al. (1999), the authors identified a more complex pattern of results. A cluster analysis in a sample of 374 university students from Germany and Austria revealed four different types of thinking styles: 1) rational: high rational and low intuitive; 2) intuitive: high intuitive and low rational; 3) complementary: high rational and high intuitive; and 4) poor – low rational and low intuitive. Further analyses showed a positive correlation between the complementary thinking style and scores on a measure of paranormal experiences. This finding indicates the importance of evaluating both intuitive and analytic thinking in the same study and taking their different patterns of interaction into consideration in the investigation of paranormal beliefs.

Even though Wolfradt et al. (1999) and Irwin and Wilson (2013) found that intuitive thinking predicted reports of paranormal experiences, the studies by Bouvet and Bonnefon (2015) and Ross et al. (2017) showed that analytic thinking style predicted only paranormal explanations for anomalous experiences but not the experiences themselves. Ross et al. (2017) suggested that such differences probably resulted from previous investigations using self-report measures of cognitive style which are less reliable in comparison to performance-based measures. Some authors have also identified an important role of gender differences, with female respondents more often evidencing an intuitive thinking style and other cognitive characteristics found to correlate with paranormal beliefs (see French and Stone, 2014, chapters two and six for a review).

In tandem with what we have seen so far with regard to paranormal beliefs, a number of scholars have also portrayed religious people as more intuitive and less analytical than atheists or skeptics (for example, Gervais and Norenzayan,

2012; Shenhav et al., 2012). Notwithstanding, Goel and Dolan (2003) and Farias et al. (2017) suggested that intuitive and analytical cognitive processes may not necessarily work in opposite ways but may coexist without mutual interference. Investigations using neuroscience paradigms and broader cultural samples (not just North American university students) have falsified the link between intuitive or analytical thinking style and religious beliefs (Farias et al., 2017; Sanchez et al., 2017; Gervais et al., 2018). Some of the explanations raised for the discrepant findings are that previous studies: 1) relied on limited cultural samples, 2) failed to evaluate intuitive and analytical thinking in the same study, 3) or overestimated the effect of analytical priming procedures on the manipulation of beliefs. In relation to cultural differences, it has been suggested that believers from secular cultures (such as the UK) are more "challenged to articulate the arguments for holding supernatural beliefs in a way that you aren't in a society where the default is to be religious [as in the U.S.]" (Farias et al., 2017, p. 3). From this perspective, the differences found might be ascribed to specific societal demands instead of a universal cognitive difference between believers and skeptics.

In all fairness, it must be acknowledged that a weak negative correlation between analytical thinking and religious beliefs have been reported by recent studies with diversified samples (e.g., Pennycook et al., 2016; Stagnaro et al., 2019). Of particular significance here is the fact that these studies focused on a limited number of beliefs (e.g., belief in God). More attention should be given in future research to other paranormal concepts and their intersection with traditional religious ideas.

3.6   Ontological Confusions

Another relevant area of investigation in relation to cognitive biases concerns what Lindeman and Aarnio (2007) called "core ontological confusions". This hypothesis assumes that people learn from early childhood to differentiate between physical, psychological, and biological phenomena. They learn, for example, that inanimate, physical objects cannot think (since they lack this psychological property) nor heal when broken (which is a biological property). These different life-domains bear specific characteristics that can be identified and differentiated. But religious and paranormal beliefs neglect such distinctive properties and instead combine elements from different domains. In psychokinesis, for example, thoughts can directly move physical objects at will, while in spiritualism, thoughts, feelings and even the whole personality are said to continue existing after bodily death. According to Lindeman et al. (2015, p. 66), these are "category mistakes where the distinctive properties of the superordinate categories of mental and physical, animate and inanimate, and living and lifeless are inappropriately mixed".

To test whether paranormal believers are more prone to such mentalizing biases, the authors devised the Core Knowledge Confusions Scale (Lindeman and Aarnio, 2007) which evaluates the extent to which certain statements (e.g., "A mind breaks when it is ill") are described by participants as metaphorical or literal. In line with the hypothesis, several studies revealed a consistent association of scores on religious and paranormal beliefs with a tendency to 'literalize' statements indicative of ontological confusions (e.g., Riekki et al., 2013; Svedholm and Lindeman, 2013; Lindeman et al., 2015). More importantly, Lindeman and Aarnio (2007) found that confusions of core knowledge discriminated believers from skeptics better than intuitive and analytical thinking.

3.7   *Delusions and Other Psychotic Symptoms*

A last research topic worth considering regarding the cognitive deficit hypothesis is the relationship between paranormal beliefs and delusions. For the purposes of this work, I define delusions as pathological beliefs – such as recurrent ideas of persecution and grandiosity – "maintained with conviction in spite of irrationality or evidence to the contrary" (American Psychiatric Association, 2015, p. 293). Many authors suggested that reasoning biases and cognitive errors underlying delusional ideation also underlie the formation of paranormal and religious beliefs (e.g., Peters et al., 1999; Lange and Houran, 1998; Lawrence and Peters, 2004; Irwin et al., 2012a, 2012b). These studies overlap considerably with the literature concerning schizotypy and psychotic experiences in the general population (e.g., Goulding, 2003; Schofield and Claridge, 2007; Peters et al., 2017; Alminhana et al., 2017).

The evidence shows that individuals reporting paranormal beliefs and experiences tend to score higher on measures of schizotypy and psychotic symptoms, albeit evidencing significantly less distress, cognitive disorganization, social anxiety, and need for care when compared with psychotic patients (e.g., Goulding, 2003; Schofield and Claridge, 2007; Peters et al., 1999, 2016; Alminhana et al., 2017). On the other hand, studies have found that believers may perform poorly on reasoning tasks, showing a propensity to cognitive biases which are characteristic of delusions (Lawrence and Peters, 2004; Irwin et al., 2012a, 2012b). For example, Lange and Houran (1998, p. 637) defined reports of poltergeist episodes as "delusions resulting from the affective and cognitive dynamics of percipients' interpretation of ambiguous stimuli", probably representing an instance of "contagious psychogenic illness". Aberrant salience – the tendency to attribute significance or importance to stimuli that would normally be considered irrelevant – was found to correlate with a measure of paranormal beliefs and experiences (Irwin et al., 2014). The neurochemical processes underpinning aberrant salience are thought to have a crucial role in the onset of psychosis (Roiser et al., 2013).

These findings are congruent with the dimensional model of psychosis which assumes that psychotic symptoms represent a series of traits distributed on a continuum. Some of these traits are healthy variations, and others, predispositions to psychosis (Peter et al., 1999). According to this model, paranormal beliefs and experiences are traits that can be found either among healthy individuals in the general population or among patients diagnosed with a psychotic disorder. In the latter case, such experiences are accompanied by suffering, disorganization, and interpersonal problems, usually requiring professional care. The major question, however, is when exactly they become pathological? Prevalence studies show that paranormal experiences are widespread across different cultures and social strata (Maraldi and Krippner, 2019), so why only a small minority of people develop psychotic disorders? There have been many attempts to establish criteria for a differential diagnosis between pathological and healthy experiences, but more research is needed to test and improve the available models (e.g., Moreira-Almeida and Cardeña, 2011; Kerns et al., 2014).

Some authors argue that cultural factors play an important role in that differentiation (Maraldi et al., 2017, 2019; Maraldi and Krippner, 2019). In a large cross-national comparison spanning 13 countries, Wüsten et al. (2018) observed that in low and middle-income countries, the endorsement rates of psychotic experiences were higher, and respondents described them as less distressing when compared to those from high-income countries. In an integrative review of the cross-cultural literature on anomalous experiences, Maraldi and Krippner (2019, p. 313) suggested that "a more fruitful approach than attempting to formulate universally valid criteria to differentiate pathological from nonpathological" experiences is "developing culturally adapted measures and definitions for positive, neutral, and negative outcomes of these experiences based on each culture's ethnoepistemology", that is, "the metaphysical and epistemological conceptions that together shape cultural beliefs and worldviews" (p. 307) – see also Kelly and Locke (2009). The authors also recommend the development of a "multidimensional perspective", encompassing genetic, interpersonal (e.g., childhood trauma, attachment patterns), sociocultural (e.g., prevalence rates, ethnoepistemology) and personality variables (e.g., schizotypy).

3.8   *Conceptual and Methodological Problems*
Overall, the reviewed studies evidence a more complex picture than initially portrayed. The findings are mixed, with some studies showing positive

correlations between cognitive biases and belief in the paranormal, while others show negative or no correlation (see also Gray and Gallo, 2016 for mixed findings from a large-scale test of the cognitive deficit hypothesis). The findings also varied according to cultural and gender differences, as well as the cognitive processes and tasks under investigation. In some experiments evaluating pattern perception sensitivity and verbal creativity, paranormal believers outperformed skeptics. Believers may be more prone to patternicity (although skeptics are not completely immune to it), but especially in relation to ambiguous stimuli.

Despite divergences, the evidence suggests that analytical thinking may coexist with belief in the paranormal. Also, the endorsement of paranormal beliefs does not necessarily decrease with more years of education (actually, it had sometimes increased), although courses specifically targeting their legitimacy were efficacious in reducing their acceptance. Finally, paranormal beliefs and experiences sometimes overlap with psychotic symptoms. Nonetheless, paranormal believers and experiencers in the general population often report less distress, social impairment and need for care when compared with psychotics. Based on a thorough review of the evidence, Irwin (2004, p. 24) concludes that "not all paranormal beliefs are delusory in a technical sense, and paranormal belief therefore should not be defined as a type of delusion".

There are important methodological problems in these studies varying from lack of ecological validity to little consideration of cultural factors. Irwin (1991) raised concerns over the fact that some of these investigations were performed by "publicly professed skeptics", whose main motivation "was to expose paranormal believers as illogical, irrational, credulous, uncritical, foolish people" (p. 289). Expressed negative attitudes toward paranormal experiences might contribute to "members of the public to be reticent about sharing their experiences with others (especially members of the health professions) for fear of seeming, at best, naïve or gullible [...] or, at worst, as suffering from some underlying psychopathology" (Roe, 2020, p. 46). The role of contextual effects and other response biases is often neglected in mental health research including the field of spirituality, religion, and health, despite substantial evidence showing that such biases may lead to false conclusions based on spurious correlations between variables and errors in prevalence rates of mental disorders (Maraldi, 2020b).

The majority of the evidence supports the occurrence of contextual and experimenter effects in research on paranormal beliefs (Fishbein and Raven, 1967; Layton and Turnbull, 1975; Crandall, 1985; Wiseman and Schlitz, 1997; Smith et al., 1998; Sparks et al., 1998; Watt and Wiseman, 2002; Ramsey, Venette and Rabalais, 2011). More specifically, these studies show with varying degrees of strength and based on diverse research paradigms that a researcher's attitude toward the paranormal may influence participants' scores on different psychological measures, significantly biasing the results. The investigation of contextual effects represents a significant issue for further research, especially given the scientific controversy surrounding paranormal phenomena.

But beyond experimenter differences, another major confounder in research on paranormal beliefs is the imprecise definition and measurement of belief in the paranormal. The Revised Paranormal Belief Scale (RPBS), the most widely used measure of paranormal beliefs, put in the same basket telepathy, the Loch Ness Monster, precognition, and omens such as black cats bring bad luck and the number 13 is unlucky (Tobacyk, 2004). Some studies have found that beliefs in cryptozoological creatures and items on bad luck do not form coherent factors, are seldom scored positively by respondents and might have different connotations for young people than for old people (Irwin, 2004; Maraldi, 2014, Lindeman et al., 2016, Maraldi and Farias, 2019). Even in the case of parapsychological concepts, the reasons for endorsing the existence of telepathy and reincarnation may not necessarily overlap. In this sense, how should we interpret the total score of the RPBS? This has been a topic of some debate in the literature (see Irwin, 2004, chapter three for a review), but no firm conclusion was drawn. Although acknowledging the multidimensionality of paranormal beliefs, most authors calculate a total score and use it to compare high and low scorers.

Based on findings from a Brazilian sample, Maraldi and Farias (2019) suggested that the total score can be construed as a measure of religious hybridism, especially if we consider that the RPBS includes both paranormal and traditional religion items. However, this may vary as a function of cultural differences. In Brazil and Latin America, for example, religious hybridism is a common and widespread phenomenon (Morello, 2019). I have also suggested elsewhere that the RPBS total score may be simply a crude measure of New Age hybridism (Maraldi, 2014). But another possible interpretation is that it reflects an unstable or confused worldview. From this perspective, a person scoring high on the RPBS total score may not clearly discriminate between spiritual beliefs, therefore applying the same standards to things such as telepathy, cryptozoological creatures, or belief in God. If this hypothesis holds true, it might explain why some studies found a relationship between paranormal belief and cognitive biases or psychopathology. For some individuals, the RPBS total score is perhaps evidencing their struggles to integrate different (and sometimes conflicting) perspectives into a personal bricolage and thus make sense of life in a liquid modernity (Bauman, 2000). This is also in accordance with findings from research on multiple religious belonging (Peres et al., 2020) and spirituality without religion (King et al., 2013), which suggest that people without stable and defined worldviews may report more psychopathological symptoms, sometimes as part of a spiritual crisis (Lukoff et al., 1992; Maraldi, 2020a).

This "liquid spirituality hypothesis" may also explain why paranormal beliefs correlate with conspiracist ideation (e.g., Darwin et al., 2011; Pennycook et al., 2015). Given their loose criterion for discriminating between spiritual worldviews and degrees of evidence, RPBS high scorers might also endorse a whole range of other ideas without filtering irrelevant or discrepant information. If God, the Loch Ness Monster, extraterrestrial beings, and astral projection are all possible, then certain intricated conspiracies may be credible too.

Finally, our hypothesis may contribute to elucidate the differences found by some investigators between New Age and traditional religiosity. For instance, Houran et al. (2001) observed that New Age beliefs (but not traditional religiosity) showed small but consistent correlations with a series of psychopathological indicators. Some authors have suggested that the psychopathological implications of religious and paranormal beliefs are better explained in terms of the strength of commitment to a group or belief system rather than the content of belief (Zuckerman et al., 2016). Members of organized religion, particularly those who attend more frequently, tend to benefit from the social support provided by the religious community (Peres et al., 2020), as well as from an increase in self-esteem and subjective well-being (Arrowood and Cox, 2020). Since New Age religiosity is more institutionally fluid, it could predispose individuals to more distress in the face of uncertainty and doubt. From this perspective, the RPBS total score is not exactly evidencing the disadvantages of belief in the paranormal *per se*, but reflecting more complex, sociohistorical phenomena associated with contemporary spirituality, especially some popular presentations of it.

If the diverse interpretations raised above for the total score show to be empirically valid, this may indicate that the mixed findings obtained by the reviewed studies were perhaps capturing different psychosocial processes as a function of sampling. Depending on the characteristics of each sample, the scenarios may change, yielding different results that reflect different individual and collective realities. In that sense, an important factor to consider here is how participants interpret scale items. Can we assume that all respondents think the same way when they respond the question: "I believe in God"? RPBS items are thought to reflect a universal construct, but this assumption obscures the hegemonic influence of Western belief systems in its development, such as Christianism and New Age esotericism. In the case of paranormal experiences, some authors have dealt with cultural biases by adjusting the wording of the items to make them more neutral and descriptive (e.g., Irwin et al., 2013; Taves et al., 2019). But since 'belief' and 'experience' are multifaceted and dynamic cultural phenomena, and not static, universal traits that vary only according to frequency or intensity, any standardized instrument that aims to capture their diversity ends up, at some point, failing in its task. I am not denying with this argument the existence of a hypothetical common core underlying different cultural presentations of paranormal beliefs and experiences; however, this over-arching pattern should emerge not from the previous imposition of culturally biased categories, but from a rigorous appreciation of the different cultural expressions that together evidence the existence of a common core. For that purpose, it is of fundamental importance to take into consideration the cultural and historical dynamics underlying paranormal beliefs and experiences. Perhaps the first step is to recognize that the influences of ideology and context cannot be fully eliminated from research (Watson, 2019).

Wiseman and Watt (2006, p. 333) suggested researchers evaluate the possibility of incorporating additional factors in paranormal belief scales "for example, reflecting the degree of conviction with such beliefs are held, and the evidence on which they are based (e.g., personal experiences, another person's experiences, media influence, religious influence ...)". Additionally, it is recommended that researchers use more rigorous procedures of translation, cross-cultural adaptation and validation including semantic validity and ideally Rasch scaling and differential item functioning analysis (Lange et al., 2018). Irwin et al. (2013) and Maraldi and Krippner (2019) suggested separating generic experiences from appraisals; in this direction, Taves et al. (2019) developed an inventory that distinguishes between the two and allow for detailed comparisons between appraisals and experiences. In addition, comparisons between subgroups of participants such as "believers but not experiencers", "experiencers but not believers", and "believers and experiencers" would allow us to detail the role of paranormal experiences in the formation of paranormal beliefs, as well as their particular networks of interrelationship with cognitive and personality variables. Also, longitudinal studies would be fundamental to understand how paranormal experiences and beliefs change over time. Finally, studies comparing individuals with different religious styles (Streib et al., 2020) in their conceptions about psychic phenomena and reports of psychic experiences could help further our understanding of the relationship between religion and the paranormal. As Laursen (2014, p. 250) once bemoaned, the psychology of the paranormal "usually resort to the simplistic and unproductive believer/non-believer dichotomy when there are far richer, pluralistic ways to examine human experiences and the (fantastical) ideas that emerge from them, as has been increasingly exemplified in interdisciplinary science and religious studies".

4   Parapsychology and Religion

It is often said that ontological issues are outside the purview of psychology and its various subdisciplines. But as seen regarding the cognitive deficit hypothesis, psychologists often ignore this and raise hypotheses that imply that certain phenomena are most likely false. To tell when our perception and reasoning are reliable or unreliable, accurate or distorted is to make an ontological judgement. It means we have (or think we have) an understanding of what is reality and how certain experiences deviate from a supposed Archimedean point – or what James Mark Baldwin (1861–1934) once named "the coefficient of external reality" (Baldwin, 1891). The fact is that "we actually know little of the fundamental structure of reality [...] and the basis of broadly accepted experiences, consciousness" (Fallon, 2015, p. x).

The cognitive deficit hypothesis is based on the assumption that "If sceptics are correct and the paranormal is not real then we should expect to find some differences in cognition or cognitive abilities between those who do and do not believe in the paranormal" (French and Stone, 2014, p. 116). This argument presupposes that the individual characteristics of believers and experiencers are important indicators of the inexistence or unreality of paranormal events. But this notion neglects the basic fact that the sun will be there, whether I believe in its existence or not, and whether my thoughts about the nature and origin of the sun are correct and substantiated by scientific evidence. Most of the world population believe today in the existence of coronavirus, albeit having no scientific knowledge and experience to substantiate their belief. Most laypeople, especially those that did not become ill or did not lose a loved one, believe in the reality of coronavirus because of the authority of scientists, the media, and the government, or because they have heard about someone else's experience with COVID-19. People may even hold unscientific beliefs about the origins, mechanisms of action, and treatment of COVID-19, but none of this makes the disease less real and less dangerous. In a similar vein, the possibility of ostensible paranormal phenomena cannot be ruled out based on cognitive bias alone. As Wiseman and Watt (2006, p. 329) observed in relation to patternicity: "believers' increased ability to find correspondences between events and experiences, and therefore to attribute psychic causation to such experiences, does not necessarily imply that such attributions are erroneous." The cognitive deficit hypothesis confuses correlation with causation and reduces an ontological problem to a psychological one. It incurs the same *ad hominem* fallacy (no matter how sophisticated) of medical materialism (the notion according to which subjective experience can be explained entirely by physiological processes), whose excesses were denounced by James (1902/2002, p. 19) more than a century ago: "In the natural sciences and industrial arts it never occurs to anyone to try to refute opinions by showing up their author's neurotic constitution. Opinions here are invariably tested by logic and by experiment, no matter what may be their author's neurological type".

French and Stone (2014, p. 119) argue that "to conclude that an event is paranormal is to decide that there is no rational explanation". The problem with this assertion is that it turns parapsychology into an instance of irrational thinking. The whole enterprise of investigating and theorizing about the possible existence of paranormal processes becomes an illusion. From this perspective, a real dialogue with parapsychology is impossible. This reasoning also confuses the definition of the 'paranormal' with the nature of the phenomenon. We call an event as "psychic" or "paranormal" because, if it is veridical, we currently do not understand (or have only a limited knowledge of) its nature and mechanisms. But the term 'paranormal' means almost nothing in relation to the event; it is merely an operational and provisory definition, a demonstration of our ignorance (the same could be said of 'psychic', 'psi', 'anomalous', or other alternative terms). Something is paranormal because it does not fit our current notions of normality, and not necessarily because it is inherently beyond our understanding. In this sense, it might be possible someday to find a rational explanation for its existence. "Parapsychology is full of descriptive terms which do no explaining, but they do have the useful function of allowing us to speak of the otherwise unspeakable" (Perry, 1987, p. 99).

Many critics of parapsychology have argued that extraordinary claims require extraordinary evidence, a motto analogous to Flournoy's Principle of Laplace: "the weight of the evidence should be proportioned to the strangeness of the facts" (Flournoy, 1990, p. 345). However, the problem lies in the definition of 'extraordinary', which is highly debatable (Cardeña, 2018). Also, care must be taken that methodological rigor does not become an excuse for the systematic and biased refusal of certain studies and researchers, merely because they investigate paranormal claims. In this respect, Greenhouse (1991) recommends that the standards of other scientific disciplines should be equally applied to parapsychology. It is worth remembering that Flournoy (1900) recommended an adequate balance between the Principle of Laplace and the Principle of Hamlet so that established theories are not inconsequently discarded, whereas innovations are also not suppressed.

In accordance with these two principles, I defend here a combination of "the virtues of Western Enlightenment thinking with its disciplined examination of evidence" and "a more expansive and all-embracing worldview that allows for seemingly impossible things", following the work of Bowie (2014, p. 20). In keeping with the initial proposal to entertain the possibility of real psychic phenomena, I ask the reader to consider for a moment the hypothesis that what people describe during these experiences is veridical (even if only partially veridical). If that is the case, how would this impact our understanding of religious and paranormal claims?

4.1 Strengths and Limitations of Personal Experience: Parapsychology's Response

As previously seen, it is often difficult (if not sometimes impossible) to demarcate a clear line between religion and the paranormal. In Spiritualism, for instance, reports of psychic phenomena are at the core of its teachings and practices. This seems to be so because religions provide experiencers with a meaning framework with which they contextualize and understand their experience. In fact, for some commentators (Lang, 1909; McClenon, 2002; Laubach, 2004), religious narratives may have initially emerged out of attempts to make sense of psychic and other exceptional experiences (including, perhaps, mystical experiences not covered by parapsychology). In support of this view is the finding that paranormal *experience* is one of the best predictors of paranormal *belief* (Irwin, 1985; Glicksohn, 1990; White, 1985, 1997; Dagnall et al., 2016; Roe, 2020). Even among parapsychologists, personal experience was found to be important to their conviction in the existence of psychic phenomena (McConnell, 1975; Irwin, 2014).

Reports of psychic events come in different shades from the more prosaic to the exceptional. In many instances, they have not only stimulated one's curiosity, as have profoundly changed one's beliefs and attitudes, including increased spirituality, religious conversion or deconversion, and positive psychological change (Greyson, 2014; Surbhi and Greyson, 2015). Psychic experiences are reported to have sometimes saved the experiencer from danger or, conversely, informed him/her about a loved one in danger (e.g., Gurney et al., 1886; Rhine, 1965; Radin, 1997, 2006). These experiences may also help people cope with suffering and bereavement, bearing important therapeutic implications (Cooper et al., 2015).

Psychological theories of religion and the paranormal have hitherto privileged what I call 'the principle of analogy'. What believers and experiencers say about such phenomena is not usually accepted as possible; their experiences and beliefs *must* point to another thing, something which is not what they imagine to be valid. But precisely because the real thing is thought to be rather different from what experiencers suppose it to be, their interpretations can only be explained as errors and illusions or, in the best-case scenario, as psychological projections. For example, in Freudian psychoanalysis, God is depicted as a symbolic representation of the exalted father, something *analogous*, but different from the metaphysical God (this view was later attenuated in psychoanalytic studies on the 'images of God', Hood, 2012). Similarly, what people believe to be psychokinesis or precognition is described as nothing more than an expression of magical ideation or fantasy proneness, an exercise in imagination, or worse, a delusion. This is not necessarily different in parapsychology; indeed, some parapsychologists explain psi phenomena in ways that do not always corroborate spiritual beliefs. But at least the experience is not dismissed beforehand as an ontological confusion or a psychological or social projection. What the experiencers and spiritual traditions say is important and help researchers develop theoretical models and experimental protocols.

This situation places parapsychologists in a delicate position. When they propose to take religious and exceptional claims seriously, they are labeled as pseudoscientists; but when their findings contradict some religious or spiritual notion, their research is described as reductionistic and limited. Parapsychology is not one thing or the other, but something in between. As sociologist Erich Goode (2000, p. 137) observed, there is a considerable gap between parapsychological experiments and the popular image of psychic phenomena:

> Most people imagine levitating gurus, infallible, mind-reading clairvoyants, spiritualists who can melt cancer away with a touch of the hand [...] The parapsychologist's assertion of obtaining experimental results that depart from statistical chance are not what the public has in mind when psychic powers are discussed or depicted. The field of parapsychology occupies a territory somewhere between the public stereotype and the scientific ideal.

An often-neglected consequence of such distinction is that the findings of psychological research on the paranormal are not necessarily generalizable to research in parapsychology. For example, participants' performance on anomalous cognition tasks may not confirm their beliefs about their own presumed psychic abilities (Nash, 1953). In a recent investigation, Delorme et al. (2020) found that controls performed better than self-defined mediums on an image classification task using photographs of deceased individuals. Although additional neurophysiological findings indicated that the mediums were possibly more stressed and less attentive during the experiment, this study illustrates how parapsychological evidence can be tricky in relation to religious/spiritual claims.

By the same token, scores on psi tasks have been demonstrated to be largely unrelated to psychopathological indicators. Psychotics and other psychiatric patients often perform at chance level, despite eventually claiming psychic abilities (Rhine, 1950; Zorab, 1957; Greyson, 1977). Some studies have found that psi performance was *negatively* correlated with neuroticism and defensiveness and *positively* associated with creativity and openness to experience (see Carpenter, 2012 for a review). Rabeyron and Watt (2010) found no significant correlation between psychopathological symptoms, childhood trauma, and stressful life events with scores on a computerized precognition task. On the other hand, spontaneous paranormal experiences did show to be associated with psychopathological variables, as in many other psychological studies.

Leaving aside for a moment the important issue of ecological validity (we shall return to it later), these experiments apparently show that there might be important differences between what people believe about their experiences and the processes underlying them. This is not new to psychologists; they have long demonstrated that this may well apply to diverse human characteristics (e.g., Nisbett and Belows, 1977; Dunning et al., 2003). In fact, we are unconscious of most of the psychological and neurophysiological processes underlying our experiences, and this is also true of psi. Some parapsychological experiments suggest that a person may be physiologically aroused apparently in response to a distant stimulus (in time or in space) without *consciously* knowing it (Radin, 2006; Braud, 2008; Cardeña, 2018). The language with which we describe psi experiences is partially misleading because it indicates conscious, accessible knowledge when in most cases people are not fully aware (if at all) of what is really happening to them (Stanford, 1974; Carpenter, 2012).

I do not intend with the above considerations to disregard the importance of personal experience. Parapsychology exists in the first place because people in different cultures report psychic events. Some parapsychologists have even suggested that a return to introspection could offer some valuable insight into "psi-in-the-living", that is, the ways whereby psychic processes (if they are genuine) manifest in everyday life including religious contexts and practices (White, 1985; Felser, 2001). Parapsychologists are both receptive and critical of paranormal allegations. They are aware of the limitations of introspection and observation and continuously search for ways to establish more controlled conditions of investigation. This greatly varies according to the allegation under consideration; for example, cases of children who spontaneously claim to remember previous lives are particularly difficult to study from an experimental paradigm. Therefore, most of the research in this area is based on prolonged observations and in-depth interviews with the child, his/her family, social entourage, and the family of the purported previous personality, involving either qualitative or quantitative analyses. Additional information might be obtained from documents, psychological testing, and medical/physical examination (Stevenson, 1980; Matlock, 2019).

In general, allegations concerning after-death communication have shown to be only partially amenable to parapsychological investigation; experimental studies may inform whether mediums or channelers provide accurate information about a deceased person under controlled conditions but have little (if anything) to say about the existence of a purported spiritual world (May and Marwaha, 2015; Maraldi, 2017). Spiritualists often rely on *ad hoc* speculation to argue in favor of survival, making their hypothesis immune to refutation (Maraldi and Krippner, 2013). Nonetheless, the allegation that some mediums apparently provide veridical information about deceased people that they could not obtain by ordinary sensory means can surely be submitted to scientific investigation, as well as the psychological, physical, and biological factors implicated in such occurrences. Indeed, studies have found that some mediums provide very accurate information about deceased persons under controlled, experimental conditions, and more often than one would expect by chance alone (Gauld, 1982; Rock, 2014). An investigation on the electrocortical activity associated with mediumship found that, as a mental process, the experience of communicating with deceased persons is distinct from various other imaginative processes, contradicting the hypothesis that psychic experiences result from fantasy (Delorme et al., 2013). Interviews and questionnaires can also be used to investigate the phenomenology of mediumistic experiences (e.g., Rock et al., 2009), as well as their cognitive and personality correlates (e.g., Roxburgh and Roe, 2011). Researchers who argue in favor of a non-materialist perspective recognize the limitations of the evidence derived from mediumship and reincarnation cases, but nevertheless, defend that these findings can be considered *suggestive* of postmortem survival (e.g., Stevenson, 1977, 1980; Kelly et al., 2007; Matlock, 2019).

If, in the popular mind and psychological research, things such as telepathy, precognition, spiritual healing, and life after death are all interconnected, parapsychology differentiates them according to 1) the extent to which they are empirically verifiable, 2) the research protocols employed to investigate them (see May and Marwaha, 2015 for a review), and 2) the strength of the evidence in their favor. Also, allegations of psychic occurrences must always be reassessed for 'normal', non-psi explanations. Even if an effect is considered by parapsychologists to have reached substantial empirical confirmation, this does not mean that every time a person reports a similar event, he/she is describing a veridical psi occurrence. William James recommended that paranormal explanations should be raised only after fraud, chance occurrence, sensory leakage, and cryptomnesia (Flournoy, 1900) were adequately addressed (Murphy and Ballou, 1960). The psychology of the paranormal is in a way embedded in parapsychology and serves as a constant reminder of the limitations of personal experience. However, it cannot fully account for parapsychological findings.

On the other hand, it would be erroneous to think that religious believers and mystics are always unaware of such psychological pitfalls. As a matter of fact, most of the training in contemplative traditions involve identifying and overcoming illusions and distractions along the way to spiritual development (Braud, 2008). Authors such as Haynes (1964) and Nicol (1976) also observe that centuries before the emergence of modern psychical research and parapsychology, many theologians had developed similar criteria and methods to differentiate between veridical and fraudulent reports of spiritual phenomena – see also Heaney (1979). In the Catholic church, the *advocatus diaboli* ("Devil's advocate"), a canon lawyer designated to take a skeptical stance toward the exceptional claims attributed to a candidate for canonization, was for many centuries a sort of religious parapsychologist, also anticipating some of the ideas further developed by modern psychologists and physicians to explain paranormal accounts such as psychopathological symptoms and errors of memory and perception. More interestingly, the devil's advocate could even differentiate between a paranormal event – in the sense of a human ability – and what was regarded to be a supernatural phenomenon resulting from divine providence or demonic influence. In relation to exorcism, Hayes (1964) observed that the traditional catholic rites prescribed that "the exorcist is to be a man who does not easily believe that possession has occurred" (p. 393).

4.2   *Parapsychologists and Religion over Time*

Given the profound historical connections between parapsychology and the study of religion, one would expect a more thorough dialogue between these two research areas. Recently, some scholars (e.g., Bowie, 2014; Kripal, 2017) have argued in favor of an approximation, but the dominant perspective is still sociohistorical and does not usually address ontological issues (e.g., Geisshuesler, 2019; Pence, 2020). From the side of parapsychologists, the topic has been poorly explored and does not feature as a prominent aspect of contemporary research.

In a survey with members of the Parapsychological Association carried out a few decades ago, Tart (2003) has found that 49% of respondents answered that spirituality was not an important motivation to enter the field, while 45% answered that it was completely or partly important. A remaining 6% were unclear. Moreover, only one third answered that their work in parapsychology is inspired by spiritual motivations, while 26% reported some conflict between their spirituality and experimental research in parapsychology. These figures seemed to indicate that spirituality was "a common, but far from dominant, reason for becoming a parapsychologist" (p. 183). Nonetheless, Tart acknowledges that he did not define 'spiritual' and many participants complained about the lack of explanation for that term. Given the strong criticism often suffered by parapsychologists, some respondents might have answered the questions in a socially desirable way, thus avoiding any connection with things spiritual. In any case, these findings illustrate how diverse parapsychologists may be in their spiritual (or non-spiritual) motivations and interests, what bear implications for the relationship between parapsychology and religion/spirituality.

Since the old days of psychical research, parapsychologists manifest a variety of backgrounds and perspectives on the existence and *modus operandi* of psychical phenomena. However, their opinions also changed over time, giving rise to different approaches to the relationship between parapsychology and religion.

When discussing the findings of his survey, Tart (2003) notes that they contradicted the assertion that parapsychologists are primarily motivated to confirm their own spiritual beliefs. But in his 1900 presidential address to the London SPR, Myers (1900) argued that although "the quest of immortality will answer to a stronger element of personal desire [...] such desire need not imply bias in the estimation of the evidence" (p. 110). From this perspective, parapsychologists' spiritual motivations are not obstacles in the way of knowledge. Quite the contrary, for Myers, the lack of this desire for immortality is actually indicative of "our race's immaturity" for "when a man cares little for existence this is because existence cares little for him, and that it has been doubt as to the value of life and love which has made the decadence of almost all civilizations" (p. 113).

But why such desire needs science? Myers explains that the evidence provided by religions is "not adequate, as standing alone, to justify conviction" and "priests have thought it safest to defend their own traditions, their own intuitions, without going afield in search of independent evidence of a spiritual world" (p. 113). For Myers, "no attachment to Christian tradition, no recognition of the need and value of high intuitions, should blind us to the fact that only truths scientifically demonstrated can a world-philosophy or world-religion be based" (p. 110). In this context, the chief purpose of psychical research is "to prove the preamble of all religions", that is, "that a spiritual world exists". Once the existence of this world is demonstrated, the theologian can "reason on that world or feel towards it" as he will (p. 117).

Myers defines psychical research as a synthesis of science and religion or, more specifically, a "wider Science, of which Religion is the subjective aspect". He appeals to theologians, arguing that "the intellectual virtues have now become necessary to salvation" and that "these virtues have grown outside the ecclesiastical pale", being necessary to strengthen them as part of an "ecumenical" and "evolutionary" perspective in dialogue with science. In this sense, Myers criticizes the spiritualists for having "transferred to certain new dogmas – for most of which they at least have some comprehensible evidence – the uncritical faith which they were actually commended for bestowing on certain old dogmas, – for many of which the evidence was at least beyond their comprehension". At the same time, he blames "people's religious instructors" – probably referring to priests and other representants of official religions – for not having trained the population to investigate "the new facts" (that is, the psychic manifestations brought about by spiritualist gatherings during the 19th century) for themselves. Here, he seems to attribute an educational purpose to psychical research, by defending that the only solution for the "weaknesses of modern spiritualism" is "teaching the mass of mankind that the maxims of the modern *savant* are at least as necessary to salvation as the maxims of the medieval saint" (Myers, 1900, p. 124).

Myers conferred to the SPR a spiritual duty: the establishment of "an age of transition" during which Psychical Research would spread all over the world, paving the way for "the coming century's leaders of spiritual thought" to completely reunite science and religion in a synthesis of the universe capable of satisfying "those questions which the human heart will rightly ask, but to which Religion alone has thus far attempted an answer" (p. 125). Thus, for Myers, the scientific purposes of Psychical Research were inseparable from their spiritual and moral purposes. The aim of this science was ultimately to correct religion, not destroy it. But he was also aware that not all of his colleagues were on his side: "I am speaking for myself alone. I am not giving utterance to any collective view" (p. 119).

Myers continues to be relatively influential among parapsychologists and his legacy has rendered several articles and books surveying his contributions. The book *Irreducible Mind* by Kelly et al. (2007) is perhaps the most prominent appraisal of his work in light of more recent investigations. But even among those who defend that there is scientific evidence suggestive of postmortem survival, their approach is different from Myers in the sense that it is more empirically grounded and less directly concerned with spiritual issues, although the narrative of reconciliation between science and spirituality is still present and surely plays a fundamental role – see, for example, Kelly et al. (2015). A similar pattern can also be observed in the history of psychology: the transition from more philosophical and all-encompassing theories to an eminently empiricist perspective.

Someone fundamental to that transition in parapsychology was certainly J. B. Rhine. Rhine was also very interested in the spiritual implications of parapsychology but was more moderate than Myers and refrained from developing a whole spiritual program, despite believing that the findings of parapsychology supported the notion that the human being has a non-physical aspect (Rhine, 1953). Rhine was much more critical of the evidence for postmortem survival and emphasized the importance of an experimental, laboratory approach, restricting research interests to what could be more objectively measured.

In contrast to Myers, who synthesized religion and science and put spirituality at the center of Psychical Research, Rhine saw parapsychology as a wider field of which the relationship with religion was very important, but not central. He introduced a specific branch for that purpose, the 'parapsychology of religion'. Rhine saw the creation of this subfield as a profitable way of parapsychologists to obtain funding for research:

> Parapsychology, even after a hundred years of more or less continuous research, has not found a market; it is still entirely dependent for its support upon philanthropy. If therefore it should prove that parapsychology can, on its own scientific level, be applied to any of the problems and needs of religion, the prospect of such usefulness would be welcomed by many parapsychologists whether or not they are especially interested to religion.
>
> RHINE, 1977–1978/1985, pp. 191–192

Rhine believed that such an exchange would be interesting to religious believers and theologians as well. He saw the situation of religions in the Western world as "critical", with increasing levels of disaffiliation and the loss of authority to science. Rhine thought that parapsychology could help religions regain receptivity. He remembered the role played by the spiritualist movement at the beginning of psychical research and acknowledged the fact that "the first general theories of parapsychological phenomena were religious in character". However, parapsychology had later to "withdraw from the very spiritualist association that had helped to generate it" in order to "follow a scholarly path" (p. 192).

But how, then, may parapsychology contribute to reinstate religions' authority? For Rhine, the principal enemy of religions is philosophical materialism "or the view that man's nature is wholly physical". By showing that phenomena such as telepathy, clairvoyance and precognition do seem to occur, parapsychologists have demonstrated that, under certain circumstances, we may transcend the usual limitations of our perception and muscular activity, reaching a realm beyond physical explanation: "it is enough for the present to say that parapsychology has in a real sense confirmed the spiritual (i.e., extra-physical) nature of man" (p. 194).

Rhine went on discussing some of the specific contributions of parapsychology to the understanding of religious beliefs. He proposed a secular explanation for the idea of God. According to him, God's attributes correspond to specific types of psi:

> The "all-seeing eye" of the divine being is equivalent to a supreme order of clairvoyance; knowledge of things to come is precognition; the searching awareness of what is in the hearts of men is telepathy, and the wondrous physical miracles that adorn the legendry of the faiths of mankind would generally conform to the concept of psychokinesis in parapsychology today.
>
> RHINE, 1977–1978/1985, p. 195

Whereas Myers (1900) used expressions such as "infinite intelligence" (p. 120), "cosmic law" (p. 126) and "ultimate energy" (p. 127), and even spoke of "God" (p. 123) and "discarnate spirits" (p. 119) apparently taken for granted their existence, Rhine stated that "the claims of mediumship [...] have never reached the point of justifiable scientific decision" (p. 193) and suggested that God is a psychological projection, a personalization of psychic abilities. His hypotheses about God thus combine psychology and parapsychology in the same explanation – see also Grosso (1985) and Braude (1997) for very similar ideas. Turning his attention to religious revelation and miracles, Rhine explains them based on the "general forms of manifestation in which psi more commonly occurs: *dreams, hallucinations, intuitions,* and *physical effects*" (Rhine, 1977–1978/1985, p. 197). The psychic processes studied at the lab differ from those reported by prophets and mystics only in terms of intensity and content. In a way similar to what has been found in the lab, "prophets and seers of religious history [...] could not just sit down and evoke their powers at will" (p. 198).

However, Rhine did not completely neglect the possibility of "a personal universe" to which human beings could turn for help during difficult moments. Religions may either "accept and use the new knowledge" provided by parapsychology or "wait until the need is better indicated" (p. 200). In any case, Rhine insisted on the existence of a "common foundation" between theological claims and parapsychology which would merit further investigation. He even suggested, "the cross-cultural analysis of religious practices in search of better psi test conditions" (p. 198).

The later generations of parapsychologists largely maintained Rhine's emphasis on the experimental approach but developed a series of new protocols over the years, going beyond card-guessing tasks, experiments with dices, and the forced-choice method. The return to (and improvement of) the free-response method used in the early days of psychical research, the use of relaxation techniques to produce mild alterations in consciousness – considered to be "psi-conducive" – as part of the Ganzfeld technique (Hyman and Honorton, 1986), the studies with random number generators, the use of physiological measurement to detect covert psi phenomena, the remote viewing protocol, and various other developments followed the Rhine era. But another interesting change occurred in terms of religious references.

Whereas Rhine and Myers thought of religion mainly in terms of Christianity and Spiritualism, contemporary parapsychologists are significantly influenced by Eastern mysticism (particularly Indian philosophical traditions) and its parallels with modern physics (e.g., Radin, 2013; Kelly et al., 2015). More recently, some authors have also incorporated insights from shamanistic practices, ancient magic, and psychedelic religions (e.g., Rock et al., 2012; Radin, 2018; Luke, 2020).

The concept of spirituality also gained prominence in recent decades. Authors such as Tart (2002, 2009) and Walach (2015) believe that research in parapsychology and related areas such as transpersonal psychology, mysticism, and consciousness studies contradict materialism and scientism and will bring forth a secular spirituality based on the union of science and the knowledge provided by different spiritual traditions from both East and West. In this sense, Walach criticizes the tendency of some transpersonal psychologists to favor Eastern traditions, ignoring the knowledge produced by Christian theologians: "If we were able to leave those dogmatic discussions aside for a moment and find consensus about the way that leads to the threshold before discussing the furnishing and the number of rooms in the house, we would have already gained a lot" (Walach, 2015, p. 104). He argues in favor of a universalist and integrative perspective that would help establish "peace between religions" (p. vii) and provide more adequate strategies to deal with issues such as fundamentalism, climate change, misery and poverty, and the meaning of life. Both Tart and Walach attach much importance to personal experience, establishing a more fluid dialogue between spirituality and experimental approaches. The focus is not on science (as in the dialogue proposed by Rhine) but on the establishment of a worldview within which science would play its role alongside spiritual traditions. Thus, their ideas seem more in tune with those of Myers.

Walach's views of religion and religiosity are heavily influenced by his focus on inner experience. He thinks of religion as an institutionalized "form of expression" for spiritual experiences and argues that religions should always change, accompanying the insights brought about by new experiences. A religion or tradition that is unable to adapt to such changes becomes "increasingly irrelevant, untimely, and hollow" (p. 25). Such criticism of traditional, organized religion as outdated and incompatible with developments in science and personal experimentation with the sacred follows parapsychology since the old days of psychical research and can also be found in the work of Myers and many others. What these authors are all attempting is to give rise to a new form of relationship with whatever we might call the divine – or, better yet, the spiritual – which is not incompatible with rationality and experience. Underlying this worldview is a search for integrating reason and emotion, personal experience and scientific experimentation; in other words, a reaction to the excesses of science without entirely disregarding science, and a reaction to religious dogmatism without disregarding religious experience. In this context, parapsychological findings "place some challenge to the mainstream [materialist] paradigm" (Walach, 2015, p. 6), thus helping bring "science and spirituality together" (Tart, 2009). This is precisely what Myers had in mind when he prophesied that "the coming century's leaders of spiritual thought" would reunite science and religion in order to respond to "those questions which the human heart will rightly ask, but to which Religion alone has thus far attempted an answer" (Myers, 1900, p. 125).

But such attempts at reuniting different religions in a single worldview apparently neglect the fact that religious believers may not agree with it, and not only because of their presumed dogmatism or fundamentalism. These proposals of an integrative synthesis fail to acknowledge the complexity of religious worldviews and the many differences between them, as well as the many levels and expressions of religiosity. They also apparently dismiss the many ethical and cultural implications of such a project or approach them only superficially. This simplistic view of religion derives in part from the lack of dialogue with areas such as Psychology of Religion and Religious Studies.

There is probably a long way before we can achieve a synthesis (Grosso, 1998). One might even question if a truly consensual synthesis or integration is at all possible. Watson (2019) provides us with important considerations on the many challenges and conditions of a dialogue between the different social actors (religious or not) regarding this debate. In what concerns parapsychology, the investigations must continue, and their philosophical – and, why not, theological – implications should be thoroughly discussed, following an open and informed perspective (Cardeña, 2014).

Researchers and theoreticians will have to deal, among other things, with the fact that not all parapsychologists hold explicit spiritual worldviews and may even think that parapsychological findings are better explained in terms of physics (based on concepts such as entanglement, non-locality, and quantum retrocausality) and biological theories rather than metaphysical or religious concepts such as a personal God. If for Rhine, the existence of ESP pointed to a spiritual aspect in the human being, most contemporary theoreticians tend to see it more in terms of an expanded view of reality in which consciousness is seen as fundamental. Even those that see parapsychology and spirituality as interconnected may explain the 'spiritual' in ways that are not metaphysical or divine. For Walach et al. (2009, p. 277), for example, spirituality is "the alignment of the individual with the whole, experientially, motivationally and in action". Nothing in their definition suggests that this "whole" is an omnipresent God or a pantheistic deity, although it could eventually be associated with the mystical experience of all-connectedness. In reviewing the evidence for the efficacy of intercessory prayer, Dossey (2005, p. 392) clearly distinguishes spirituality from religion. Although recognizing the religious implications of this research (for example, when acknowledging patients' religiosity in clinical practice), he opposes the view according to which research on intercessory prayer presupposes the existence of God or a transcendental realm:

> Another common criticism is that these studies are metaphysical; they invoke a transcendent agency or higher power, which places them outside the domain of empirical science. This is a straw-man argument, because researchers in this field make no assertions about entelechies, gods, or metaphysical agents in interpreting their findings. They are searching for correlations between intentions and observable effects in the world. Nearly always they defer on the question of mechanism, which is an accepted strategy within science.

A similar debate can be observed in relation to research on postmortem survival. Rhine's cautionary notes on the survival hypothesis and his emphasis on experimental research may have contributed to reduce the interest of parapsychologists in Myers' quest of immortality, even though research in this area continued to attract some attention over the twentieth century (Gauld, 1982). In recent decades, this situation has significantly changed, and various studies emerged dealing specifically with the issue of survival (e.g., Beischel, 2007; Braude, 2003; Kelly et al., 2007; Rock, 2014). In a survey with members of the Parapsychological Association, Irwin (2014) found that more than half of participants agreed that survival research is essential to the field. Still, some investigators argue that this research area is unlikely to really answer the metaphysical question of survival after death (Irwin, 2002; Krippner and Hövelmann, 2005) and is "problematical" (May and Marwaha, 2015, p. 2) with regard to evidence showing that anomalous cognition is sufficient to explain the veridical information obtained during mediumship, reincarnation, out-of-body, and near-death experiences. On the other hand, the defendants of the survival hypothesis point to the specificity of their evidence, arguing that the phenomena they study are related to psi but are not completely reducible to it (Rock, 2014). Greyson (2007), for instance, considered mental clarity, vivid sensory imagery, and clear memory for near-death episodes as common features of these experiences, hardly explainable under general anesthesia, cardiac arrest or other similar conditions involving altered cerebral physiology. For him, "this continuation and even enhancement of mental functioning at a time when the brain is physiologically impaired present problems for the mind-brain identity model" (p. 140). It should be added that, although survival after death is typically conceptualized in terms of post-Cartesian forms of interactive dualism, Kelly et al. (2015) have also suggested alternative explanatory models based on idealism or a neutral or dual-aspect monism – see also Kastrup (2019).

Regardless of the conclusion of this interesting debate, there might still be room for reconciliation between parapsychology and religion. The history of religions shows us that they eventually learned to recognize the contributions of science, and even found ways to incorporate scientific findings into their own activities and theological conceptions. This should not be different in the case of parapsychology. In their turn, parapsychologists should not only acknowledge the contributions of religious traditions but learn to accept their own limitations. They might come to realize, as did Servadio (1985, p. 5) that: "Perhaps the manifestations surrounding the mystics may enable us to glimpse an aspect of reality for which our standard methods of studying and assessing natural phenomena are not suitable". The fact is that, despite taking exceptional experiences seriously, parapsychology is not immune from some of the same ontological challenges faced by psychology of religion and religious studies. In this sense, parapsychologists should remain open to the possibility that there is "some ontological entity [for example, God] hidden somewhere in the recesses of Being" (Grosso, 1985, p. 39) and that "Psi may simply be one way in which God or the transcendent or the Divine reveals itself in our world" (p. 162).

4.3   Psi and Religious Variables

Although the implications of parapsychological findings for religion and spirituality were many times discussed over the history of parapsychology, few studies have actually investigated the relationship between psi and religious or spiritual variables. Further investigation in this direction could help answer the question of whether psi is fundamentally related to religiosity and spirituality or only partially connected to them. In what follows, I will provide a review of this literature and suggest some possible areas for further inquiry.

A first line of investigation concerns the correlation between psi perfor-mance and variables such as self-reported religiosity and religious beliefs. In this direction, Nash (1953) found that ESP scores were positively and signifi-cantly correlated with an original measure of "religious values". No informa-tion on the questionnaire items, validity, and reliability was provided, though. In a series of eight ESP experiments, Haraldsson (1993) used three original measures: 1) a combined measure of religiosity – including four questions tap-ping self-reported religiosity, religious reading, frequency of prayer, and reli-gious attendance –; 2) a measure of religious beliefs – covering items on belief in God, reading of the bible, and self-reported religiosity –, and 3) a single-item measure of belief in the afterlife. He found that both the combined measure of religiosity and belief in the afterlife significantly correlated with ESP scores in two of the experiments and for all the experiments combined. Religiosity showed to be a better correlate of ESP when compared with belief in psychic phenomena since psychic belief evidenced more contradictory findings and nonsignificant results.

These are interesting findings in view of studies showing that belief in psychic ability (not necessarily the person's own psychic abilities, but psy-chic ability in general) is an important predictor of psi. This has been named by experimental psychologist Gertrude Schmeidler (1912–2009) as 'the sheep-goat effect'. Schmeidler (1945) took the terms *sheep* and *goat* from the New Testament:

> When the Son of Man comes in his glory, and all the angels with him, he will sit on his glorious throne. All the nations will be gathered before him, and he will separate the people one from another as a shepherd separates the sheep from the goats. He will put the sheep on his right and the goats on his left.
>
> MATTHEW 25:31–33

For Schmeidler, the sheep symbolizes the believer while the goat symbolizes the unbeliever. Carpenter (2012, p. 279) explains that "the effect of sheep scor-ing above chance in ESP tests and goats scoring below is relatively robust, and it has been found in many studies using several variations on the measure". But some studies also found contradictory results in relation to the sheep-goat effect – see Cardeña et al. (2015) for a recent review. However, the studies by Nash and Haraldsson indicate that religiosity rather than belief in psychic ability is a better predictor of psi. Interestingly, this was not further explored, despite evidence suggesting that taking participants' religiosity into consideration and adapting the experiment to address their beliefs might enhance psi performance (e.g., Giesler, 1985).

It is recommended that parapsychologists use standard measures of religiosity, spirituality, and mysticism already employed by psychologists of religion. Constructs such as religious development, intrinsic and extrinsic religiosity, attachment to God, and daily spiritual experiences could be investigated in relation to psi performance in different experiments. It would also be of relevance to compare religious and non-religious participants, as well as individuals with different levels of religious involvement from leaders to followers. This would eventually help parapsychologists find novel correlates for psi and identify significant relations between their experimental findings and everyday experiences and practices. Also, the experimenter's religiosity should be considered in the analysis and discussion of the evidence, especially in the light of previous investigations demonstrating the occurrence of experimenter effects in psi research and the psychology of the paranormal (see Palmer and Millar, 2015 for a review).

Another central aspect of religious life is the relationship between the faithful and a transcendent being or god(s). This relationship is frequently one of worship and fear, but also of appeal. Religious believers often seek God's help through prayer in order to deal with difficult situations, as well as protect and save them or their loved ones from danger. Similarly, in many spiritual practices, people are said to be able to influence the physical and mental state of others by means of intention, even at a distance. In parapsychology, these different claims are often subsumed under the category of *noncontact healing* including practices such as intercessory prayer, reiki, spiritist passes, and many others. The extant findings suggest that it is often difficult to rule out the placebo effect as a likely explanation, but studies investigating the role of distant intention in the behavior of other animals, plants and microorganisms provide significant evidence for the existence of this phenomenon (Cardena, 2018). Radin et al. (2015) offer some important methodological recommendations for future research. Several studies on the psychological aspects of prayer had been conducted by psychologists of religion (Spilka and Ladd, 2013) and parapsychologists could eventually benefit from this literature to improve ecological validity and measurement of variables related to prayer and distant intention in different religious contexts.

The report of psychic occurrences in religious contexts usually centers around gifted individuals. As Thouless (1971, p. 86) has remarked, psychic phenomena are very often regarded as "signs [...] of the holiness of the person producing the event". Various mystics and religious figures from Jesus to Sri

Ramakrishna were said to be able to anticipate the thoughts of other persons in a way that would seem today to involve psi processes. But although experimental research has frequently found that there are individuals who tend to score higher than others, there is virtually no evidence suggesting that psi can be produced on demand (Cardeña, 2018). Still, the use of selected participants showed to be efficacious, giving support to the idea that most psychic processes seem to depend on an individual predisposition. Although the belief of an individual in his/her own psychic abilities may not be a good predictor of psi, religious groups may eventually help researchers identify participants that seem to be more predisposed to obtain better 'hit rates'. It is recommended that researchers develop their research protocols in collaboration with the members of the religious groups under investigation and adjust the design to approximate the conditions expected for the phenomena to occur, without losing sight of experimental controls and data reliability.

Although not producible on demand, psychic occurrences are nevertheless facilitated by certain conditions. When in an altered state of consciousness elicited by techniques such as hypnosis, meditation or relaxation, participants tend to perform better in psi experiments, as exemplified by the Ganzfeld technique. This is in accordance with the many instances of religious, spiritual, and shamanistic practices devised to intentionally modify the normative state of consciousness (e.g., fasting, hyperventilation, psychedelic substances, contemplative practices) and facilitate the occurrence of psychic and mystical experiences. Different studies suggest that long-term practice of meditation is linked to enhanced psi performance (Cardeña, 2019). The evidence also shows that alterations in consciousness induced by Yoga, meditation, and religious rituals might enhance psychophysiological functioning and control, allowing for phenomena such as heart rate control, bleeding control, reduced metabolism, enhanced perceptual sensitivity and creativity (Servadio, 1985; Kelly et al., 2007; Cardeña, 2020). The consideration of these studies by psychologists of religion may point to other relevant factors implicated in religious experiences and beliefs beyond basic cognitive mechanisms and psychosocial variables.

Psi experiments have typically obtained small effect sizes. Part of this problem derives from the fact that experimental conditions may lack ecological validity. It is widely recognized in parapsychology that anecdotal reports of psi in everyday life are usually much more intense and impactful. If this is considered by some to be evidence that such narratives are exaggerated and does not indicate veridical events, it is also possible that parapsychological experiments are failing to reproduce the necessary conditions for psi to manifest in its fullness. Although parapsychologists have tried for many times to create more ecologically valid experiments with the use of games and the evaluation of psi functioning in contexts such as casinos and religious rituals (Radin, 1997; Hirukawa et al., 2006), this has not necessarily solved the issue of small effect sizes – but see Cardeña (2018) for a discussion of effects of similar magnitude in other scientific disciplines. Could the dialogue between parapsychology and psychology of religion and spirituality help improve ecological validity in relation to experiments involving religious variables, practices, and groups? This is a question worth considering in future investigations.

A final word should be said regarding the construct of *transliminality*, which is considered by some to unify both the psychological research on mystical and paranormal experiences and the findings of parapsychology. The term 'Transliminality' was coined by Michael Thalbourne (1955–2010) who initially defined it as "an opening or receptiveness to impulses and experiences whose sources are in preconscious (or unconscious) processes" (Thalbourne, 1991). The concept has evolved, and other definitions were tentatively proposed (Thalbourne et al., 1997). Transliminality is currently defined as a "hypothesized tendency for psychological material to cross thresholds into or out of consciousness" (Lange et al., 2000). The roots of the concept of transliminality can be traced back to Myers' notion of the "subliminal self" (Myers, 1903), as well as to James' examination of religious experiences (James, 1902/2002). The word transliminality derives from the Latin terms *trans* (to cross) and *limen* (threshold), border (Thalbourne, 2000a).

Thalbourne (2009) argued that individuals who evidence prominent levels of transliminality will show a greater permeability for mental contents to cross the threshold between conscious and unconscious states. Such contents may appear in different forms including phenomena such as hyperesthesia, fantasy proneness, openness to experience, dream interpretation proneness, absorption in nature and in art, and paranormal beliefs and experiences (Lange et al., 2000; Thalbourne, 2000a).

Transliminality is assessed by the Rasch-scaled Revised Transliminality Scale (or RTS). The RTS showed to be unrelated to social desirability and intelligence (Thalbourne et al., 1997) and demonstrated good cross-cultural validity (Lange et al., 2018). The scale showed to be of clinical relevance including evidence of positive and significant correlations with dissociation (Thalbourne, 1998), schizotypy (Dagnall et al., 2010; Fleck et al., 2008), reports of childhood trauma (Thalbourne et al., 2003), memory dysfunctions (Houran and Thalbourne, 2003), and lability of the temporal lobes (Thalbourne et al., 2003, 2008). Another important correlate is the creative personality (Thalbourne, 2000b), which is closely linked to psychopathology (Thalbourne and Delin, 1994). Transliminality is also of interest to research concerning religiosity and mystical experiences (Thalbourne and Delin, 1994, 1999). Thalbourne and

Delin (1999) found that transliminality was significantly and positively correlated with both mystical experiences and religiosity, especially "a more nontraditional, esoteric, or experiential" religiosity (p. 52).

Thalbourne and colleagues proposed that the neurophysiological basis of transliminality can be explained in terms of a facilitated cortical activation due to a greater permeability of the sensory membrane, which could result in a weak suppression of irrelevant information, thereby creating a fusion of sensory experiences. Such sensory fusion would result from the hyperconnectivity of limbic-temporal structures with sensory association cortices, which might explain why transliminality is usually correlated with anomalous sensory experiences as synesthesia. This sensorial fusion would also comprise the basis of other perceptual experiences such as hyperesthesia (Thalbourne et al., 2003). Similarly, Evans et al. (2019, p. 418) suggested that transliminality is an expression of "neuroplasticity, that is, an enhanced interconnectedness between brain hemispheres, as well as among frontal cortical loops, temporal-limbic structures and primary or secondary sensory areas or sensory association cortices".

Although the described mechanism is believed to exist in every individual, its action threshold is hypothesized to vary from one person to another. In support of this model, experimental studies have found evidence for an enhanced vibrotactile sensibility in people with high scores on the transliminality scale (Houran et al., 2006). A significant, positive correlation was also found between transliminality and performance accuracy in a visual detection task involving subliminal priming (Crawley et al., 2002).

In what concerns psi, studies employing different experimental paradigms have found that transliminality significantly predicted psi performance (e.g., Storm and Thalbourne, 1998–1999; Del Prette and Tressoldi, 2005). However, Parker (2000), Rabeyron and Watt (2010) and Rock et al. (2012) failed to replicate this finding.

Transliminality is an all-encompassing construct that promises to integrate research in parapsychology and psychology, as well as the contributions of the founding fathers with the more empiricist approach characteristic of our times. But it remains unclear whether the RTS score really reflects the concept hypothesized by Thalbourne and colleagues. The concept of transliminality initially emerged from a series of factor analyses indicating the existence of a single factor underlying the relationship between different variables. Thalbourne and colleagues refined the concept until finally describing it as "a tendency for psychological material to cross thresholds into or out of consciousness", a definition inspired by the works of Myers and James. However, Maraldi (2014) suggested that transliminality might be best viewed as a measure of paranormal /

mystical experiences and their main correlates in the popular mind, probably reflecting the "liquid spirituality" already discussed in part three. The evidence that the RTS significantly predicted vibrotactile sensitivity and visual accuracy tend to confirm Thalbourne's hypothesis, but more research is needed to demonstrate its hypothesized neurophysiological basis. That said, I see transliminality as a promising concept to which both parapsychologists and psychologists of religion should devote their attention and maybe work together to explore it and improve it.

5   Concluding Remarks

The aims of this work were to discuss how parapsychological findings may inform research on religious/spiritual experiences, and whether a dialogue between parapsychology and psychology of religion is possible. I began with a brief review of the history of psychical research / parapsychology, pointing out its connections with the history and development of modern psychology and the circumstances that have set these research fields apart. After presenting my own views regarding this historical controversy (in the introduction part) and discussing some fundamental terminological and conceptual issues in parapsychology and psychology (in part two), I dedicated the third part to a critical review of the psychological literature on the paranormal. In particular, I defended that this field became less a scientific endeavor and more an ideological program devised to denigrate paranormal believers and experiencers. In assessing the evidence bearing on the cognitive deficit hypothesis, I argued that it reveals a confused pattern of findings and several methodological and conceptual problems. This hypothesis also lacks sensitivity to alterity and diversity. It downplays and pathologizes the Other including not only paranormal believers in Western societies but by extension many non-western cultures and indigenous communities where the paranormal is actually normal and pervades their worldviews in ways that would lead us to assume, if this hypothesis is accepted, that entire cultures are "weird", "fallacious", "confused", or "pathological". I also discussed alternative explanations for the reviewed findings and made recommendations for future research.

In part four, I developed the notion that parapsychological research may inform our understanding of religious/spiritual experiences by fostering a more open-minded, sensible perspective toward the explanations offered by religious and paranormal believers/experiencers. In this sense, I showed that the findings of research on the psychology of the paranormal cannot always be generalized to research in parapsychology. I defended a conceptual shift from belief to experience and discussed both the strengths and limitations of the latter, showing how parapsychology responds to such limitations through systematic observation and experimentation. Next, I went on to review the complex relations between parapsychology and religion over time, surveying the variety of perspectives embraced by parapsychologists and their implications for a dialogue with religion and spirituality. Finally, I reviewed the evidence for the relationship between psi and religious variables, emphasizing the need for parapsychologists to address the contributions of the psychology of religion in their studies.

A common argument against parapsychology is that it is a religion rather than a scientific discipline. But we saw that its relationship with religion is ambiguous, with some findings apparently contradicting religious beliefs. Also, certain religious claims remain currently beyond the possibility of parapsychological investigation (e.g., the existence of God and a spiritual world). Moreover, some of the attempts of parapsychologists to explain religious beliefs are based on natural processes such as psychological motivations and biological evolution rather than theological or metaphysical concepts. For most parapsychologists, psi is a human ability that has eventually helped humans survive and reproduce, not a divine or spiritual gift (e.g., Broughton, 2015) – see also Potts and Devanno (2013) for a discussion of materialist perspectives in parapsychology. Even those that defend a post-materialist paradigm and the importance of research on postmortem survival do not simply reiterate *in totum* what religions say about reincarnation and the afterlife.

But despite this complex scenario, parapsychological findings do provide evidence in favor of phenomena that most religious people experience as genuine, even if such findings do not neatly fit their experiences and convictions. Even though parapsychologists still could not come up with an integrative, consensual theory for psi, their findings have been consistently replicated and showed coherent patterns of relationship with different psychological and social variables including religiosity. An expanded and open-minded psychology of religion should therefore take these findings into consideration. However, I am not asking psychologists of religion to accept them without question, but at least to entertain their possibility. I would like this work to start the debate and not resolve it, especially because much more can still be said regarding the role of religious variables in psi performance.

For this debate to be possible, we cannot look to religions only as practices or beliefs. We must also consider the prominent role of experience. Entire spiritual traditions were born out of revelatory experiences reported by their founders – prophetic dreams, apparitions, spiritual healing, to name just a few examples. These experiences form the basis of the moral teachings, rituals, and symbols of many religions. Shushan (2016) argued, for example, that near-death accounts served as the basis for many native American afterlife beliefs and religious revitalization movements. Some of the powerful narratives inspired by psychic experiences eventually transcended the local communities where they originated, reaching the status of worldwide religions and philosophies. Contemporary spiritual movements follow a similar path (even if they are not always named 'religions'), gathering around certain spiritual narratives a growing number of adherents (Taves, 2016).

We can define religions, at least in part, as sophisticated ideological traditions and practices devised to explain and exert control over certain experiences (including psychic experiences), as well as reflect on their moral and existential consequences, establishing standards of conduct in life and in the relationship with the forces or agents reportedly revealed by them. I say "in part" because I do not want to neglect the importance of sociohistorical and cultural factors. Religions are, to a great extent, social constructions, but constructions need not only be "narratives" in the sense of stories about other stories. I endorse here what Porpora (2006, p. 58) has defined as "a revised social constructionism that acknowledges that objects of our experience are not all entirely constructed socially". In essence, "that means not to rule out tout court what people say they are experiencing", since "in any proper experience, the object of experience contributes something to the content of experience. The object in other words is part of what explains the content". If we were to consider that religious experience is never genuine, then "the very category of experience dissolves" (Porpora, 2006, p. 59).

I argue that reports of psychic experiences are not mere illusions and comprise fundamental cornerstones of religious narratives. Psychic accounts may be either reinforced by religions or rejected as heresy. Religious traditions often establish criteria for determining what is genuinely divine and beneficial or otherwise demonic, harmful, or even innocuous. Religious beliefs and practices both influence the phenomenology, frequency, and intensity of psychic accounts, as well as are decisively influenced by them. Still, allegations of paranormal occurrences are not exclusive of religions; they may develop even in the context of religious disbelief or a privatized, independent spirituality (Laubach, 2004).

But where these experiences originate from? For most psychologists and social scientists, they should be understood against the background of historical, political, economic, geographical, psychological, and biological forces acting upon them. Ontological issues are left for theologians and philosophers, but only as long as methodological agnosticism does not succumb to militant atheism. But we have also seen that we cannot completely avoid ontological issues and that psychologists are always making ontological judgements, which is the case with the psychology of the paranormal.

Part of the reluctance to entertain the possibility of psychic phenomena derives from the belief that, if they are real, their existence would disconfirm all the knowledge already produced by psychology and behavioral sciences. But there is no evidence to support this claim. Quite the contrary, the evidence suggests that psi is significantly associated with physiological and psychological variables and is facilitated by certain mental states such as dreaming. Psychic occurrences are also profoundly shaped by individual and cultural differences (Rhine, 1965). They may even get unnoticed in data from standard psychological experiments (Bem, 2011). If such phenomena as psychokinesis and precognition may contradict commonsensical expectations about reality, being described by some as category mistakes or ontological confusions, modern physical theories and concepts (from entanglement to retrocausality) provide some plausibility to them, even if more work is needed to demonstrate a direct association (Radin, 2006; Cardeña, 2018). As Myers' old definition of 'supernormal' suggests, much of what is considered supernatural might not be beyond nature and/or scientific explanation after all.

It follows from all this discussion that the divide between parapsychology and psychology of religion is more ideological than properly scientific. They share a common history and some of the same areas of inquiry. Also, the two disciplines are subjected to some of the same ontological challenges. Psychology of religion evidently covers a wider field regarding religious topics. But the more limited interests of parapsychologists can be explained mainly in terms of the selection imposed by experimental studies. Their research is focused on certain allegations that showed to be more amenable to experimental scrutiny such as precognition. This approach differs, however, from the work of the founding fathers of psychology and psychical research, which had a much wider scope both theoretically and methodologically. Thus, the distinction between these fields does not seem to depend on fundamental epistemological differences. It results – as many historians have argued – from the boundary-work devised to establish psychology as a natural science. However, such boundary-work contradicts the fact already pointed out by Taves (2014) that researchers from both fields may ascribe different meanings to experiences that are "very similar in terms of their underlying phenomenology" (p. 394).

As I hope to have demonstrated, the possibility of psi phenomena does not necessarily contradict methodological agnosticism. Despite advancing a bit further the debate on ontological factors possibly underpinning religious/spiritual experiences, parapsychology cannot simply "prove" that religions are true. But parapsychology does seem to show that there are more to religious experience than just analogies or projections, cognitive biases, and social and psychodynamic motivations. Although psychologists of religion sometimes concede that there might be some basis for what religious believers and experiencers say – for example, in relation to the efficacy of religious rituals (e.g., Charles et al., 2020) –, such attempts do not usually parallel the more controversial and daring efforts of parapsychologists in the investigation of ontological issues. Save for this difference, the two fields are far from being fundamentally antagonistic and the many parallels drawn throughout this monograph suggest that a dialogue is not only possible but desirable.

In conclusion, the answer to the disconfirmation of Freud and Leuba's prediction should be searched not in a presumed failure of science to purge irrationality from our societies, but in the religious and paranormal experiences themselves. In this context, parapsychological research suggests that such experiences cannot be completely reduced to psychological needs and motivations (even though they are deeply related to them). Their presumed veracity and the potential to transform people's lives and worldviews should be equally addressed. I hope this work has contributed to show that ontological issues are worth considering by psychologists of religion, despite the many challenges on the way.

Acknowledgment

I would like to thank Carlos Alvarado and Lisette Coly from Parapsychology Foundation for providing some useful references used in this work.

References

Aarnio, Kia and Marjanna Lindeman (2005). Paranormal beliefs, education and thinking styles. *Personality and Individual Differences* 39: 1227–1236.

Alcock, James (1981). *Parapsychology: Science or magic? A psychological perspective.* Elmsford, New York: Pergamon Press.

Alcock, James (1987). Parapsychology: Science of the anomalous or search for the soul? *Behavioral and Brain Sciences* 10: 553–565.

Alcock, James and Laura Otis (1980). Critical thinking and belief in the paranormal. *Psychological Reports* 46: 479–482.

Aleti, Mario, Alessandro Antonietti and Daniela Vilani (2019). The psychology of religion and its surroundings: some trends and themes. In: *International Association for* the Psychology of Religion Conference in Gdansk, Poland – Psychology of Religion and Spirituality: New Trends and Neglected Themes, Program and Abstracts, p. 42.

Alvarado, Carlos (2002). Dissociation in Britain during the late nineteenth century: The Society for Psychical Research, 1882–1900. Journal of Trauma and Dissociation 3(2): 9–33.

Alvarado, Carlos (2006). The term 'Parapsychology'. Parapsychology Foundation Lyceum Blog #9, March 16. Available at: http://www.pflyceum.org/111.html.

Alvarado, Carlos (2014). G. Stanley Hall on Mystic or Borderline Phenomena. Journal of Scientific Exploration 28(1): 75–93.

Alvarado, Carlos (2020). Dissociation and the Unconscious Mind: Nineteenth-Century Perspectives on Mediumship. Journal of Scientific Exploration 34: 537–596.

American Psychological Association (2015). APA dictionary of Psychology (2 ed.). Washington, DC: American Psychological Association.

Arrowood, Robert and Cathy Cox (2020). Terror Management Theory: A Practical Review of Research and Application. Religion and Psychology 2: 1–83.

Askevis-Leherpeux, Françoise (1990). Croyance au surnaturel et instruction. Communications 52: 161–174.

Asprem, Egil (2010). Parapsychology: Naturalising The Supernatural, Re-Enchanting Science. In: Handbook of Religion and the Authority of Science (Brill Handbooks on Contemporary Religion, vol. 3). Jim R. Lewis and Olav Hammer (eds). Leiden, The Netherlands: Brill, pp. 633–670.

Alminhana, Letícia Oliveira, Miguel Farias, Gordon Claridge, Claude Robert Cloninger and Alexander Moreira-Almeida (2017). Self-directedness predicts quality of life in individuals with psychotic experiences: A 1-year follow-up study. Psychopathology 50: 239–245.

Aubrée, Marion and François Laplantine (1990). La Table, Le Livre et Les Espirits: naissance, évolution et atualité du mouvement social spirite entre France et Brésil. Paris: Jean Claude Lattès.

Bader, Christopher, Joseph Baker and Andrea Molle (2012). Countervailing forces: Religiosity and paranormal belief in Italy. Journal for the Scientific Study of Religion 51:705–20.

Baker, Joseph and Scott Draper (2010). Diverse supernatural portfolios: Certitude, exclusivity, and the curvilinear relationship between religiosity and paranormal beliefs. Journal for the Scientific Study of Religion 49:413–24.

Baker, Joseph, Christopher Bader and Frederick Carlson Mencken (2016). A bounded affinity theory of religion and the paranormal. Sociology of Religion: A Quarterly Review 77: 334–358.

Baldwin, James Mark (1891). The coefficient of external reality. Mind 16: 389–392.

Baruš, Imants and Julia Mossbridge (2017). Transcendent mind: rethinking the science of consciousness. Washington, DC: American Psychological Association.

Bauman, Zygmunt (2000). *Liquid Modernity.* Cambridge: Polity Press.

Bazak, Jacob (1972). *Judaism and Psychical Phenomena: A Study of Extrasensory Perception in Biblical, Talmudic, and Rabbinical Literature in the Light of Contemporary Parapsychological Research.* New York: Garrett Publications.

Beauregard, Mario, Gary Schwartz, Lisa Miller, Larry Dossey, Alexander Moreira-Almeida, Marilyn Schlitz, Rupert Sheldrake and Charles Tart (2014). Manifesto for a post-materialist science. *Explore* 10: 272–274.

Beischel, Julie (2007). Contemporary methods used in laboratory-based mediumship research. *The Journal of Parapsychology* 71: 37–68.

Belzen, Jacob A. (2012). *Psychology of Religion: autobiographical accounts.* New York: Springer.

Bem, Daryl (2011). Feeling the future: Experimental evidence for anomalous retroactive influences on cognition and affect. *Journal of Personality and Social Psychology* 100: 407–425.

Bensley, Alan, Scott Lilienfeld, Krystal Rowan, Christopher Masciocchi and Florent Grain (2019). The generality of belief in unsubstantiated claims. *Applied Cognitive Psychology* 34:16–28.

Blackmore, Susan and Emily Troscianko (1985). Belief in the paranormal: Probability judgements, illusory control, and the chance baseline shift. *British Journal of Psychology* 76: 459–468.

Blackmore, Susan and Rachel Moore (1994). Seeing things: visual recognition and belief in the paranormal. *European Journal of Parapsychology* 10: 91–103.

Blackmore, Susan (1997). Probability misjudgment and belief in the paranormal: A newspaper survey. *British Journal of Psychology* 88: 683–689.

Blanco, Fernando and Barberia Matute (2015). Individuals Who Believe in the Paranormal Expose Themselves to Biased Information and Develop More Causal Illusions than Nonbelievers in the Laboratory. *PLOS ONE* 10: e0131378.

Boy, Daniel and Guy Michelat (1986). Croyances aux parasciences: dimensions sociales et culturelles. *Revue Française de Sociologie* 27: 175–204.

Bouvet, Romain and Jean-François Bonnefon (2015). Non-reflective thinkers are predisposed to attribute supernatural causation to uncanny experiences. *Personality and Social Psychology Bulletin* 41: 955e961.

Boudry, Maarte, Stefaan Blancke and Massimo Pigliucci (2015). What makes weird beliefs thrive? *The epidemiology of pseudoscience. Philosophical Psychology* 28: 1177–1198.

Bowie, Fiona (2014). Believing Impossible Things: Scepticism and Ethnographic Enquiry. In: *Talking with the spirits: ethnographies from between the worlds.* Jack Hunter and David Luke (eds). Brisbane, Australia: Daily Grail Publishing, pp. 19–56.

Boyer, Pascal (1994). *The naturalness of religious ideas: A cognitive theory of religion.* University of California Press.

Braswell, Gregory, Karl Rosengren and Howard Berenbaum (2011). Gravity, God and ghosts? Parents' beliefs in science, religion, and the paranormal and the encouragement of beliefs in their children. *International Journal of Behavioral Development* 36: 99–106.

Braud, William (2008). Patanjali Yoga and Siddhis: Their Relevance to Parapsychological Theory and Research. In: *Handbook of Indian Psychology*. Koneru Ramakrishna Rao, Anand Paranjpe and Ajit Dalal (eds). Cambridge: Cambridge University Press, pp. 217–24.

Braude, Stephen (1997). Some thoughts on parapsychology and religion. In: *Body, Mind, Spirit: Exploring the parapsychology of spirituality*. Charles Tart (ed). Charlottesville, VA: Hampton Roads Publishing Company, pp. 118–127.

Braude, Stephen (2003). *Immortal remains: the evidence for life after death*. New York: Rowman and Littlefield.

Broch, Henri (2000). Save our science: the struggle for reason at the university. *Skeptical Inquirer* 24: 34–39.

Broughton, Richard (2015). Psi and biology: An evolutionary perspective. In: *Parapsychology: A handbook for the 21st century*. Etzel Cardeña, John Palmer and David Marcusson-Clavertz (eds). McFarland & Co, pp. 139–148.

Brugger, Peter, Theodor Landis and Marianne Regard (1990). A sheep-goat effect in repetition avoidance: Extrasensory perception as an effect of subjective probability? *British Journal of Psychology* 81: 455–468.

Brugger, Peter, Marianne Regard and Theodor Landis (1991). Belief in extrasensory perception and illusory control: A replication. *Journal of Psychology* 125: 501–502.

Brugger, Peter, Marianne Regard, Theodor Landis, Denise Krebs and Joseph Niederberger (1994). Coincidences: Who can say how meaningful they are? In: *Research in parapsychology*. E. W. Cook & D. L. Delanoy (eds). Metuchen, NJ: Scarecrow Press, pp. 94–98.

Bunge, Mario (1987). Why parapsychology cannot become a science. *Behavioral and Brain Sciences* 10: 576–577.

Bunge, Mario (1991). A skeptic's beliefs and disbeliefs. *New Ideas in Psychology* 9: 131–149.

Bunge, Mario (2010). *Matter and mind: a philosophical inquiry*. Heidelberg, Netherlands: Springer.

Cardeña, Etzel (2014). A call for an open, informed study of all aspects of consciousness. *Frontiers in Human Neuroscience* 8: 5–8.

Cardeña, Etzel (2015). Eminent people interested in psi. In: *Psi Encyclopedia*. The Society for Psychical Research (ed.). London: Society for Psychical Research. Available at: https://psi-encyclopedia.spr.ac.uk/articles/eminent-people-interested-psi.

Cardeña, Etzel (2018). The experimental evidence for parapsychological phenomena: A review. *American Psychologist* 73: 663–677.

Cardeña, Etzel (2019). Meditation, Exceptional Psychophysiological Control, and Parapsychology. In: *The Oxford Handbook of Meditation*. Miguel Farias, David Brazier and Mansur Lalljee (eds). Oxford: Oxford University Press.

Cardeña, Etzel (2020). Derangement of the senses or alternate epistemological pathways? Altered consciousness and enhanced functioning. *Psychology of Consciousness: Theory, Research, and Practice* 7: 242–261.

Cardeña, Etzel, John Palmer and David Marcussom-Clavertz (2015). *Parapsychology: a handbook for the 21st century*. North Caroline: McFarland & Company.

Cardeña, Etzel, Steven Jay Lynn and Stanley Krippner (2014). *Varieties of Anomalous Experiences: examining scientific evidence* (2 ed.). Washington, DC: American Psychological Association.

Carpenter, James (2012). *First sight: ESP and parapsychology in everyday life*. New York: Roman and Littlefield.

Carrington, Hereward (1907). *The physical phenomena of Spiritualism*. Boston: H. B. Turner & Co.

Casanova, José (2007). Rethinking secularization: a global comparative perspective. *The Hedgehog Review* 6: 7–22.

Castro, Madeleine, Roger Burrows and Robin Wooffitt (2014). The paranormal is (still) normal: The sociological implications of a survey of paranormal experiences in Great Britain. *Sociological Research Online*, 19: 30–44.

Cattell, James McKeen (1896). Psychical Research. *Psychological Review* 3: 582–583.

Čavojová, Vladimíra, Jakub Šrol and Marek Jurkovič (2020). Why should we try to think like scientists? Scientific reasoning and susceptibility to epistemically suspect beliefs and cognitive biases. *Applied Cognitive Psychology* 34: 85–95.

Charles, Sarah, Valerie van Mulukom, Miguel Farias, Jennifer Brown, Romara Delmonte, Everton de Oliveira Maraldi, Leon Turner, Fraser Watts, Joseph Watts and Robin Dunbar (2020). Religious rituals increase social bonding and pain threshold. *PsyArXiv* doi:10.31234/osf.io/my4hs.

Cicero, David, Aaron Neis, Mallory Claunig and Christi Trask (2017). The Inventory of Psychotic-Like Anomalous Self-Experiences (IPASE): Development and Validation. *Psychological Assessment* 29: 13–25.

Clark, Jerome (1993). *Encyclopedia of strange and unexplained physical phenomena*. Detroit: Gale Research Inc.

Coon, Deborah (1992). Testing the limits of sense and science: American experimental psychologists combat spiritualism, 1880–1920. *American Psychologist* 47(2): 143–151.

Cooper, Cal, Christopher Roe and Graham Mitchell (2015). Anomalous Experiences and the Bereavement Process. In: *Death, Dying, and Mysticism. Interdisciplinary Approaches to the Study of Mysticism*. T. Cattoi and C. M. Moreman (eds). New York: Palgrave Macmillan, pp. 117–131.

Crandall, James (1985). Effects of favorable and unfavorable conditions on the psi missing displacement effect. *Journal of the American Society for Psychical Research* 79: 27–38.

Crawley, Susan, Christopher French and Steven Yesson (2002). Evidence for transliminality from a subliminal card guessing task *Perception* 31: 887–892.

Dagnall, Neil, Andrew Parker and Gary Munley (2007). Paranormal belief and reasoning. *Personality and Individual Differences* 43: 1406–1415.

Dagnall, Neil, Gary Munley, Andrew Parker and Kenneth Drinkwater (2010). Paranormal belief schizotypy, and transliminality. *The Journal of Parapsychology* 74: 117–135.

Dagnall, Neil, Kenneth Drinkwater, Andrew Parker and Peter Clough (2016). Paranormal experience, belief in the paranormal and anomalous beliefs. *Paranthropology* 7: 4–14.

Daher, Jorge, Rodolfo Furlan Damiano, Alessandra Lucchetti, Alexander Moreira-Almeida and Giancarlo Lucchetti (2017). Research on the possibility of consciousness beyond the brain: A bibliometric analysis of global scientific output. *Journal of Nervous and Mental Disease* 205: 37–47.

Darwin, Hannah, Nick Neave and Joni Holmes (2011). Belief in conspiracy theories. The role of paranormal belief, paranoid ideation and schizotypy. *Personality and Individual Differences* 50: 1289–1293.

Dein, Simon (2016). Attitudes towards spirituality and other worldly experiences: An online survey of British humanists. *Secularism and Nonreligion* 5: 1–8.

Del Prete, Guido and Patrizio Tressoldi (2005). Anomalous cognition in hypnagogic state with OBE induction: An experimental study. *Journal of Parapsychology* 69: 329–339.

Delorme, Arnaud, Julie Beischel, Leena Michel, Mark Boccuzzi, Dean Radin and Paul J. Mills (2013). Electrocortical activity associated with subjective communication with the deceased. *Frontiers in Psychology* 4: 834.

Delorme, Arnaud, Cédric Cannard, Dean Radin and Helane Wahbeh (2020). Accuracy and neural correlates of blinded mediumship compared to controls on an image classification task. *Brain and Cognition* 146: 105638.

Dossey, Larry (2005). Spirituality, Prayer, and Medicine: What Is the Fuss Really About? *Virtual Mentor: Ethics Journal of the American Medical Association* 7: 390–394.

Donizzetti, Ana Rosa and Giovanna Petrillo (2017). Validation of the Paranormal Health Beliefs Scale for adults. *Health Psychology Open* 4: 1–8.

Doyle, Arthur Conan (1926). *The history of Spiritualism* (Vol. 1–2). London: Cassell and Company.

Dunning, David, Kerri Johnson, Joyce Ehrlinger and Justin Kruger (2003). Why people fail to recognize their own competence. *Current Directions in Psychological Science* 12: 83–87.

Durkheim, Emile (1912). *Les formes élémentaires de la vie religieuse: le système totémique en Australie*. Paris: F. Alcan.

Emmons, Charles and Jeff Sobal (1981). Paranormal beliefs: functional alternatives to mainstream religion? *Review of religious research* 22: 301–312.

Epstein, Seymour (1994). Integration of the cognitive and the psychodynamic unconscious. *American Psychologist* 49: 709–724.

Evans, Jonathan and Keith Frankish (2009). *In two minds: Dual processes and beyond*. Oxford, UK: Oxford University Press.

Evans, James, Rense Lange, James Houran and Steven Jay Lynn (2019). Further psychometric exploration of the transliminality construct. *Psychology of Consciousness: Theory, Research, and Practice* 6: 417–438.

Evrard, Renaud (2013). Psychopathologie et expériences exceptionnelles: une revue de la littérature. *L'évolution Psychiatrique* 78: 155–176.

Evrard, Renaud, Claudie Massicotte and Thomas Rabeyron (2017). Freud as a psychical researcher: the impossible Freudian legacy. *IMÁGÓ Budapest* 6: 9–32.

Fallon, James (2015). Foreword. In: *Extraordinary perception: support, skepticism, and science* (Vol. 1: history, controversy, and research, pp. IX–XV). Edwin May and Sonali Bhatt Marwaha (eds). Santa Barbara: Praeger.

Farias, Miguel and Mansur Lalljee (2008). Holistic Individualism in the Age of Aquarius: Measuring Individualism/Collectivism in New Age, Catholic, and Atheist/Agnostic Groups. *Journal for the Scientific Study of Religion* 47: 277–289.

Farias, Miguel, Valerie van Mulukom, Guy Kahane, Ute Kreplin, Anna Joyce, Pedro Soares, Lluis Oviedo, Mathilde Hernu, Karolina Rokita, Julian Savulescu and Riikka Mottonen (2017). Supernatural belief is not modulated by intuitive thinking style or cognitive inhibition. *Scientific Reports* 7: 15100.

Felser, Joseph (2001). Philosophical sensitives and sensitive philosophers: gazing into the future of parapsychology. *International Journal of Parapsychology* 12: 53–82.

Fishbein, Martin and Bertram Raven (1967). The AB scales: An operational definition of belief and attitude. In: *Readings in attitude theory and measurement*. Martin Fishbein (ed.). New York: Wiley, pp. 183–189.

Fitzpatrick, Oney and Scott Shook (1994). Belief in the paranormal: does identity development during the college years make a difference? An initial investigation. *The Journal of Parapsychology* 58: 315–329.

Flannelly, Kevin, Harold Koenig, Christopher Ellison, Kathleen Galek and Neal Krause (2006). Belief in life after death and mental health: findings from a national survey. *The Journal of Nervous and Mental Diseases* 194: 524–529.

Fleck, Jessica, Deborah Green, Jennifer Stevenson, Lisa Payne, Edward Bowden, Mark Jung-Beeman and John Kounios (2008). The transliminal brain at rest: baseline EEG, unusual experiences, and access to unconscious activity. *Cortex* 44: 1353–1363.

French, Christopher (2001). Why I study anomalistic psychology. *The Psychologist*, 14: 356–7.

French, Christopher and Anna Stone (2014). *Anomalistic psychology: exploring paranormal belief and experience*. London: Red Globe Press.

Freud, Sigmund (1924). Obsessive acts and religious practices. In: *The standard edition of the complete psychological works of Sigmund Freud* (Vol. 9). James Strachey (ed.). London: Hogarth, pp. 115–128. (Original work published in 1907)

Freud, Sigmund (1953a). Psychoanalysis and telepathy. In: *Psychoanalysis and the occult*. Georges Devereux (ed.). London, UK: International University Press, pp. 56–68 (Original work published in 1921.)

Freud, Sigmund (1953b). Dreams and telepathy. In: *Psychoanalysis and the occult*. Georges Devereux (ed.). London, UK: International University Press, pp. 69–86 (Original work published in 1922.)

Flournoy, Théodore (1900). *Des Indes à la Planète Mars: étude sur un cas de somnambulisme avec glossolalie*. Paris: Félix Alcan.

Flournoy, Théodore (1903). *Les Principes de la Psychologie Religieuse*. Geneva: H. Kundig. (Original work published in 1902).

Flournoy, Théodore (1911). *Esprits et médiums: mélanges de métapsychique et de psychologie*. Genebra: H. Kündig.

Fox, John (1992). The structure, stability, and social antecedents of reported paranormal experiences. *Sociological Analysis* 53: 417–31.

Gauld, Alan (1982). *Mediumship and survival: a century of investigations*. London: Heinemann.

Geisshuesler, Flavio (2019). A Parapsychologist, an Anthropologist, and a Vitalist Walk into a Laboratory: Ernesto de Martino, Mircea Eliade, and a Forgotten Chapter in the Disciplinary History of Religious Studies. *Religions* 10: 304.

Genovese, Jeremy (2005). Paranormal beliefs, schizotypy, and thinking styles among teachers and future teachers. *Personality and Individual Differences* 39: 93–102.

Gervais, Will and Ara Norenzayan (2012). Analytic thinking promotes religious disbelief. *Science* 336: 493–496.

Gervais, Will, Michiel van Elk, Dimitris Xygalatas, Ryan McKay, Mark Aveyard, Emma Butchel, Ilan Dar-Nimrod, Eva Kundtová Klocová, Jonathan Ramsay, Tapani Riekkia, Annika Svedholm-Häkkinena and Joseph Bulbulia (2018). Analytic atheism: A cross-culturally weak and fickle phenomenon? *Judgment and Decision Making* 13: 268–274.

Glicksohn, Joseph (1990). Belief in the paranormal and subjective paranormal experience. *Personality and Individual Differences* 11: 675–683.

Goode, Erich (2000). *Paranormal beliefs: a sociological introduction*. Illinois: Waveland Press.

Goulding, Anneli (2005). Healthy schizotypy in a population of paranormal believers and experients. *Personality and Individual Differences* 38: 1069–1083.

Gianotti, Lorena, Christine Mohr, Diego Pizzagalli, Dietrich Lehmann and Peter Brugger (2001). Associative processing and paranormal belief. *Psychiatry and Clinical Neurosciences* 55: 595–603.

Giesler, Patric (1985). Differential micro-PK effects among Afro-Brazilian cultists: Three studies using trance-significant symbols as targets. *The Journal of Parapsychology* 49: 329–366.

Gray, Stephen and David Gallo (2016). Paranormal psychic believers and skeptics: A large-scale test of the cognitive differences hypothesis. *Memory & Cognition*, 44: 242–261.

Greeley, Andrew (1975). *The sociology of the paranormal: A reconnaissance.* London, United Kingdom: Sage.

Greeley, Andrew (1995). The persistence of religion. *CrossCurrents* 45: 24–41.

Greenhouse, Joel (1991). Comment: Parapsychology – On the margins of science. *Statistical Science* 6: 386–389.

Greyson, Bruce (1977). Telepathy in mental illness: deluge or delusion? *The Journal of Nervous and Mental Disease* 165: 184–200.

Greyson, Bruce (2007). Commentary on 'Psychophysiological and cultural correlates undermining a survivalist interpretation of near-death experiences. *Journal of Near-Death Studies* 26: 127–146.

Greyson, Bruce (2014). Near-death experiences. In: *Varieties of anomalous experience: Examining the scientific evidence,* 2nd ed. Etzel Cardeña, Steven Jay Lynn and Stanley Krippner (eds). Washington, DC: American Psychological Association, pp. 333–368.

Griffin, David Ray (1997). *Parapsychology, philosophy, and spirituality: a postmodern exploration.* New York: State University of New York.

Grosso, Michael (1985). The God idea: a parapsychological perspective. In: *Parapsychology, philosophy, and religious concepts: proceedings of an international conference held in Rome, Italy.* Betty Shapin and Lisette Coly (eds). New York: Parapsychology Foundation, pp. 146–166.

Grosso, Michael (1998). The future of a synthesis: the relevance of parapsychology to religion. *The Journal of Religion and Psychical Research* 21: 1–13.

Gurney, Edmund, Frederic Myers and Frank Podmore (1886). *Phantasms of the living* (Vol. 1). London: Trübner.

Hacking, Ian (1988). Telepathy: Origins of Randomization in Experimental Design. *Isis* 79: 427–451.

Hall, Granville Stanley (1909). Mystic or Borderline Phenomena. In: *Proceedings of the Southern California Teacher's Association: Sixteenth Annual Session.* Redlands, CA: Redlands Review Press, pp. 103–107.

Hall, Trevor (1964). *The strange case of Edmund Gurney.* London: Gerald Duckworth.

Hanegraff, Wouter (1996). *New age religion and western culture: Esotericism in the mirror of secular thought.* New York, NY: E. J. Brill.

Haraldsson, Erlendur (1993). Are religiosity and belief in an afterlife better predictors of ESP performance than belief in psychic phenomena? *The Journal of Parapsychology* 57: 259–273.

Haraldsson, Erlendur (1985). Representative national surveys of psychic phenomena: Iceland, Great Britain, SWEDEN, USA and Gallup's multinational survey. *Journal of the Society for Psychical Research* 53: 145–158.

Haraldsson, Erlendur and J. M. Houtkooper (1991). Psychic experiences in the multinational human values study. *Journal of the American Society for Psychical Research* 85: 145–165.

Hardy, Alister (1979). *The spiritual nature of man.* Oxford, UK: Clarendon Press.

Haynes, Renée (1964). Catholic views of parapsychology. *International Journal of Parapsychology* 389–406.

Heaney, John (1979). Some implications of parapsychology for theology. *Theological Studies* 40: 474–494.

Hergovitch, Andreas and Martin Arendasy (2005). Critical thinking ability and belief in the paranormal. *Personality and Individual Differences* 38: 1805–1812.

Hergovitch, Andreas, Reinhardt Schott and Martin Arendasy (2005). Paranormal belief and Religiosity. *The Journal of parapsychology* 69: 293–303.

Hillstrom Elizabeth and Melissa Strachan (2000). Strong commitment to traditional Protestant religious beliefs is negatively related to beliefs in paranormal phenomena. *Psychological Reports* 86:183–189.

Hodges, R. D. and A. M. Scofield (1995). Is spiritual healing a valid and effective therapy? *Journal of the Royal Society of Medicine* 88: 203–207.

Hood Jr., Ralph Wilbur (1975). The construction and preliminary validation of a measure of reported mystical experience. *Journal for the Scientific Study of Religion* 14: 29–41.

Hood Jr., Ralph Wilbur (2012). The history and current state of research on psychology of religion. In: *The Oxford Handbook of Psychology and Spirituality.* L. J. Miller (ed.). Oxford: Oxford University Press, pp. 7–20.

Hood Jr., Ralph Wilbur, Peter Hill and Bernard Spilka (2018). *The psychology of religion: an empirical approach (fifth edition).* New York: The Guilford Press.

Houran, James, Harvey Irwin and Rense Lange (2001). Clinical relevance of the two factor Rasch version of the Revised Paranormal Belief Scale. *Personality and Individual Differences* 31: 371–382.

Houran, James and Michael Thalbourne (2003). Transliminality correlates positively with aberrations in memory. *Perceptual and Motor Skills* 96: 1300–1304.

Houran, James, Larry Hughes, Michael Thalbourne and Peter Delin (2006). Quasi-experimental study of transliminality, vibrotactile thresholds, and performance speed. *Australian Journal of Parapsychology* 6: 54–80.

Hufford, David (1982). *The terror that comes in the night: An experience-centered study of supernatural assault traditions*. Philadelphia, PA: University of Pennsylvania Press.

Huguelet, Phillip and Harold Koenig (2007). *Religion and spirituality in psychiatry*. New York: Cambridge University Press.

Hunter, Jack (2015). Between Realness and Unrealness: Anthropology, Parapsychology and the Ontology of Non-Ordinary Realities. *Diskus: The Journal of the British Association for the Study of Religions* 17: 4–20.

Hyman, Ray and Charles Honorton (1986). A joint communique: the psi ganzfeld controversy. *The Journal of Parapsychology* 50: 351–364.

Irwin, Harvey (1985). A study of measurement and correlates of paranormal belief. *Journal of the American Society for Psychical Research* 79: 301–326.

Irwin, Harvey (1991). Reasoning skills of paranormal believers. *The Journal of Parapsychology* 55: 281–300.

Irwin, Harvey (2002). Is scientific investigation of postmortem survival an anachronism? The demise of the survival hypothesis. *Australian Journal of Parapsychology* 2: 19–27.

Irwin, Harvey (2004). *The psychology of paranormal belief*. New York: Parapsychology Foundation.

Irwin, Harvey (2014). The views of parapsychologists: a survey of members of the Parapsychological Association. *Journal of the Society for Psychical Research* 78: 85–101.

Irwin, Harvey and June Young (2002). Intuitive versus reflective processes in the formation of paranormal beliefs. *European Journal of Parapsychology* 17: 45–53.

Irwin, Harvey and Caroline Watt (2007). *An introduction to Parapsychology (5th ed.)*. Jefferson: McFarland.

Irwin, Harvey, Neil Dagnall and Kenneth Drinkwater (2012a). Paranormal Belief and Biases in Reasoning Underlying the Formation of Delusions. *Australian Journal of Parapsychology* 12: 7–21.

Irwin, Harvey, Neil Dagnall and Kenneth Drinkwater (2012b). Paranormal Beliefs and Cognitive Processes Underlying the Formation of Delusions. *Australian Journal of Parapsychology* 12: 107–126.

Irwin, Harvey and Krissy Wilson (2013). Anomalous Experiences and the Intuitive-Experiential Style of Thinking. *Journal of the Society for Psychical Research* 77: 65–77.

Irwin, Harvey, Neil Dagnall and Kenneth Drinkwater (2013). Parapsychological experience as anomalous experiences plus paranormal attribution: A questionnaire based on a new approach to measurement. *The Journal of Parapsychology* 77: 39–53.

Irwin, Harvey, Malcolm Schofield and Ian Baker (2014). Dissociative tendencies, sensory-processing sensitivity and aberrant salience as predictors of anomalous experiences and paranormal attributions. *Journal of the Society for Psychical Research* 78:193–206.

James, William (2002). *The Varieties of Religious Experience: A Study in Human Nature (Centenary Edition)*. London: Routledge. (Original work published in 1902)

Jastrow, Joseph (1900). *Fact and fable in psychology*. Boston: Houghton, Mifflin and Company.

Jastrow, Joseph (1961). Autobiography. In: *A history of psychology in autobiography (Vol.1)*. Murchison (ed.). New York: Russell & Russell, pp. 135–162. (Original work published 1930)

Jones, Warren (1977). Belief in the Paranormal Scale: An objective instrument to measure belief in magical phenomena and causes. *Catalog of Selected Documents in Psychology.* Washington DC: American Psychological Association, 7, 100 (MS. No. 1577).

Kahneman, Daniel (2003). A perspective on judgment and choice: Mapping bounded rationality. *American Psychologist* 58: 697–720.

Kant, Immanuel (1766). *Dreams of a spirit seer illustrated by dreams of metaphysics.* New York: The Macmillan Co.

Kastrup, Bernardo (2019). *The idea of the world: a multi-disciplinary argument for the mental nature of reality*. Hampshire, UK: Iff Books.

Kelly, Edward, Emily Williams Kelly, Adam Crabtree, Alan Gauld, Michael Grosso and Bruce Greyson (2007). *Irreducible Mind: Toward a Psychology for the 21st Century*. New York: Rowman and Littlefield.

Kelly, Edward, Adam Crabtree and Paul Marshall (2015). *Beyond physicalism: toward reconciliation between science and spirituality*. New York: Rowman and Littlefied.

Kelly, Edward and Rafael Locke (2009). *Altered states of consciousness and psi: An historical survey and research prospectus (Parapsychology Monograph Series No. 18)*. New York, NY: Parapsychology Foundation.

Kennedy, James, Huggahali Kanthamani and John Palmer (1994). Psychic and spiritual experiences, health, well-being and meaning in life. *The Journal of Parapsychology* 58: 353–383.

Kerns, John, Nicole Karcher, Chitra Raghavan and Howard Berenbaum (2014). Anomalous experiences, peculiarity, and psychopathology. In: *Varieties of Anomalous Experiences: examining scientific evidence* (2 ed.). Etzel Cardeña, Steven Jay Lynn and Stanley Krippner (eds.). Washington, DC: American Psychological Association, pp. 175–212.

King, Michael, Louise Marston, Sally McManus, Terry Brugha, Howard Meltzer and Paul Bebbington (2013). Religion, Spirituality and Mental Health: Results from a National Study of English Households. *The British Journal of Psychiatry* 202: 68–73.

Knapp, Krister Dylan (2017). *William James: Psychical Research and the challenge of modernity*. Chapel Hill: The University of North Carolina Press.

Korpan, Connie, Gay Bisanz, Jeffrey Bisanz and John Henderson (1997). Assessing literacy in science: Evaluation of scientific news briefs. *Science Education* 81: 515–532.

Kripal, Jeffrey (2010). *Authors of the Impossible: the paranormal and the sacred*. Chicago: The University of Chicago Press.

Kripal, Jeffrey (2012). Mind Matters: Esalen's Sursem group and the ethnography of consciousness. In: *What Matters? Ethnographies of value in a not so secular age*. Courtney Bender and Ann Taves (eds.). New York: Columbia University Press, pp. 215–247.

Kripal, Jeffrey (2017). Introduction: Reimagining the super in the study of religion. In: *Religion: Super religion*. Jeffrey J. Kripal (ed.). Farmington Hills, MI: Macmillan, pp. xv–xlviii.

Krippner, Stanley and Gerd Hövelmann (2005). The future of psi research: Recommendations in retrospect. In: *Parapsychology in the twenty-first century: Essays on the future of psychical research*. Michael Thalbourne and Lance Storm (eds). Jefferson, NC: McFarland, pp. 167–188.

Krippner, Stanley and Mark Schroll (2014). Differentiating Experiences from Events, and Validity from Authenticity in the Anthropology of Consciousness. *Paranthropology* 5: 5–14.

Kurtz, Paul (1996). Two sources of unreason in democratic society: the paranormal and religion. *Annals of the New York Academy of Sciences* 775: 493–504.

Lang, Andrew (1909). *The making of religion*. London: Longmans, Green, and Co.

Lange, Rense and James Houran (1998). Delusion of the paranormal: a haunting question of perception. *Journal of Nervous and Mental Disease* 186: 637–645.

Lange, Rense, Michael Thalbourne, James Houran and Lance Storm (2000). The revised transliminality scale: reliability and validity data from a Rasch top-down purification procedure. *Consciousness and cognition* 9: 591–617.

Lange, Rense, Everton de Oliveira Maraldi, Wellington Zangari, Vanessa Corredato, Fatima Regina Machado and Carlos Alvarado (2018). A cross-cultural validation of the Revised Transliminality Scale in Brazil. *Psychology of Consciousness: Theory, Research, and Practice* 5: 414–424.

Lange, Rense, Robert Ross, Neil Dagnall, Harvey Irwin, James Houran and Kenneth Drinkwater (2019). Anomalous experiences and paranormal attributions: psychometric challenges in studying their measurement and relationship. *Psychology of Consciousness: Theory, Research, and Practice* 6: 346–358.

Latour, Bruno (2005). Thou Shall Not Freeze-Frame or How Not to Misunderstand the Science and Religion Debate. In: *Science, religion and the human experience*. Proctor (ed.). Oxford: Oxford University Press, pp. 27–48.

Laubach, Marty (2004). The social effects of psychism: spiritual experience and the construction of privatized religion. *Sociology of Religion* 65: 239–263.

Laursen, Christopher (2014). Book review: Anomalistic Psychology: exploring paranormal belief and experience by Christopher French and Anna Stone. *Journal of the Society for Psychical Research* 78: 249–251.

Lawrence, Emma and Emmanuelle Peters (2004). Reasoning in believers in the paranormal. *Journal of Nervous and Mental Disease* 192: 727–733.

Layton, Bruce and Bill Turnbull (1975). Belief, evaluation, and performance on an ESP task. *Journal of Experimental Social Psychology* 11: 166–179.

Leonard, Carrie Ann (2014). *Fallacious beliefs: gambling specific and belief in the paranormal* (Doctoral dissertation, Department of Psychology). Alberta, Canada: University of Lethbridge.

Leuba, James Henry (1916). *The belief in God and Immortality: a psychological, anthropological and statistical study*. Boston: Sherman, French & Company.

Lindeman, Marjanna and Kia Aarnio (2007). Superstitious, magical, and paranormal beliefs: An integrative model. *Journal of Research in Personality* 41: 731–744.

Lindeman, Marjanna and Annika Svedholm (2012). What's in a Term? Paranormal, Superstitious, Magical and Supernatural Beliefs by Any Other Name Would Mean the Same. *Review of General Psychology* 16: 241–255.

Lindeman, Marjanna, Sandra Blomqvist and Mikito Takada (2012). Distinguishing Spirituality from Other Constructs: Not a Matter of Well-Being but of Belief in Supernatural Spirits. *Journal of Nervous and Mental Disease* 200: 167–173.

Lindeman, Marjanna, Annika Svedholm-Häkkinen and Jari Lipsanen (2015). Ontological confusions but not mentalizing abilities predict religious belief, paranormal belief, and belief in supernatural purpose. *Cognition* 134: 63–76.

Lindeman, Marjanna, Annika Svedholm-Häkkinen and Tapani Riekki (2016). Skepticism: Genuine unbelief or implicit beliefs in the supernatural? *Consciousness and Cognition* 42: 216–228.

Loewenthal, Kate Miriam (2018). The OCD – religion package: might it relate to the rise of spirituality? *Mental Health, Religion & Culture* 21:123–130.

Lynn, Steven Jay (2017). Anomalous, exceptional, and nonordinary experiences: Expanding the boundaries of psychological science. *Psychology of Consciousness* 4: 1–3.

Luke, David (2020). Anomalous psychedelic experiences: at the neurochemical juncture of the humanistic and parapsychological. *Journal of Humanistic Psychology* online first publication.

Lukoff, David, Francis Lu and Ronald Turner (1992). Toward a More Culturally Sensitive DSM–IV: Psychoreligious and Psychospiritual Problems. *Journal of Nervous and Mental Disease* 180: 673–682.

MacDonald, Douglas (2000) Spirituality: Description, Measurement, and Relation to the Five-Factor Model of Personality. *Journal of Personality* 68: 153–197.

MacDonald, Douglas, Harris Friedman, Jacek Brewczynski, Daniel Holland, Kiran Kumar Salagame, Krishna Mohan, Zuzan Gubrij and Hye Wook Cheong (2015). Spirituality as a Scientific Construct: Testing its Universality Across Cultures and Languages. *PLOS ONE* 10: e0117701.

Majima, Yoshimasa, Alexander Walker, Martin Harry Turpin and Jonathan Fugelsang (2020). Culture as a Moderator of Epistemically Suspect Beliefs. OSF. June 10. osf. io/cbfwj.

Maraldi, Everton de Oliveira (2014). *Dissociação, crença e identidade: Uma perspectiva psicossocial* [*Dissociation, belief and identity: A psychosocial perspective*]. Doctoral thesis, University of São Paulo, São Paulo, Brazil.

Maraldi, Everton de Oliveira (2017). Letter to the editor: The scientific investigation of anomalous self and identity experiences. *Journal of Nervous and Mental Disease* 205:11.

Maraldi, Everton de Oliveira (2020a). Spirituality and wellbeing: is there a necessary link? Toward a critical approach to the study of spirituality. In: *Spirituality and Wellbeing: Interdisciplinary Approaches to the Study of Religious Experience and Health*. Bettina Schmidt and Jeff Leonardi (eds). Sheffield: Equinox Publishing Home, pp. 19–43.

Maraldi, Everton de Oliveira (2020b). Response bias in research on religion, spirituality, and mental health: a critical review of the literature and methodological recommendations. *Journal of Religion and Health* 59: 772–783.

Maraldi, Everton de Oliveira, Fatima Regina Machado and Wellington Zangari (2011). Importance of a psychosocial approach for a comprehensive understanding of mediumship. *Journal of Scientific Exploration* 24:181–196.

Maraldi, Everton de Oliveira, Wellington Zangari, Fatima Regina Machado and Stanley Krippner (2014). Anomalous mental and physical phenomena of Brazilian mediums: a review of the scientific literature. In: *Talking with the spirits: ethnographies from between the worlds*. Jack Hunter and David Luke (eds). Brisbane, Australia: Daily Grail Publishing, pp. 257–299.

Maraldi, Everton de Oliveira, Stanley Krippner, Maria Cristina Monteiro Barros, Alexandre Cunha (2017). Dissociation from a cross-cultural perspective: implications of studies in Brazil. *Journal of Nervous and Mental Disease* 205: 558–567.

Maraldi, Everton de Oliveira and Carlos Alvarado (2018). Final chapter, From India to the Planet Mars: A Study of a Case of Somnambulism with Glossolalia, by Théodore Flournoy (1900). *History of Psychiatry* 29(1): 110–125.

Maraldi, Everton de Oliveira Maraldi, Fatima Regina Machado and Wellington Zangari (2018). In defense of a critical (but sympathetic) view of the anomalous. *Mindfield* 10: 61–65.

Maraldi, Everton de Oliveira and Stanley Krippner (2019). Cross-cultural research on anomalous experiences: Theoretical issues and methodological challenges. *Psychology of Consciousness: Theory, Research, and Practice* 6: 306–319.

Maraldi, Everton de Oliveira, Ricardo Nogueira Ribeiro and Stanley Krippner (2019). Cultural and group differences in mediumship and dissociation: exploring the varieties of mediumistic experiences. *International Journal of Latin-American Religions* 3: 170–192.

Maraldi, Everton de Oliveira and Miguel Farias (2020). Assessing Implicit Spirituality in a non-WEIRD Population: Development and Validation of an Implicit Measure of New Age and Paranormal Beliefs. *The International Journal for the Psychology of Religion* 30: 101–111.

Marks, Anthony, Donald Hine, Rebecca Blore and Wendy Phillips (2008). Assessing individual differences in adolescents' preference for rational and experiential cognition. *Personality and Individual Differences* 44: 42–52.

Marshall, Joey and Daniel Olson (2018). Is 'Spiritual but Not Religious' a Replacement for Religion or Just One Step on the Path Between Religion and Nonreligion? *Review of Religious Research* 60: 503–518.

Martín, Eloísa (2017). Peter Berger's Theory of Secularization in Latin America: The Two Sacred Canopies. *Journal of the American Academy of Religion* 85: 1137–1146.

Mathijsen, François (2009). Empirical Research and Paranormal Beliefs: Going Beyond the Epistemological Debate in favor of the Individual. *Archive for the Psychology of Religion* 31: 319–333.

Matlock, James (2019). *Signs of Reincarnation: Exploring Beliefs, Cases, and Theory.* New York: Roman and Littlefield.

May, Edwin and Sonali Bhatt Marwaha (2015). *Extrasensory perception: support, skepticism, and science* (Vols. 1–2). Santa Barbara: Praeger.

McClenon, James (2002). *Wondrous healing: shamanism, human evolution, and the origin of religion.* Illinois: Northern Illinois University Press.

McConnell, Robert (1975) The motivations of parapsychologists. *Journal of the American Society for Psychical Research* 69: 273–280.

Menezes Jr., Adair, Letícia Alminhana and Alexander Moreira-Almeida (2012). Sociodemographic and anomalous experiences profile in subjects with psychotic and dissociative experiences in religious groups. *Archives of Clinical Psychiatry* 39: 203–207.

Mill, Davina, Thomas Gray and David Mandel (1994). Influence of Research Methods and Statistics Courses on Everyday Reasoning, Critical Abilities, and Belief in Unsubstantiated Phenomena. *Canadian Journal of Behavioural Science* 26: 246–258.

Miller, Jon (1987). The Scientifically Illiterate. *American Demographics* 9: 27–31.

Miller, Lisa (2012). *The Oxford Handbook of Psychology and Spirituality.* Oxford: Oxford University Press.

Moreira-Almeida, Alexander and Etzel Cardeña (2011). Differential diagnosis between non-pathological psychotic and spiritual experiences and mental disorders: A contribution from Latin American studies to the ICD-11. *Brazilian Journal of Psychiatry* 33(Suppl 1): 29–36.

Morello, Gustavo (2019). Why study religions from a Latin American sociological perspective? An introduction to religious issue, 'religion in latin america, and among latinos abroad'. *Religions* 10:1–12.

Murphy, Gardner and Robert Ballou (1960). *William James on Psychical Research*. New York: The Viking Press.

Murken, Sebastian (2019). How shall we speak of God? The principle of the exclusion of the transcendent revisited. In International Association for the Psychology of Religion Conference in Gdansk, Poland – Psychology of Religion and Spirituality: New Trends and Neglected Themes, Program and Abstracts, pp. 41–42.

Musch, Jochen and Katja Ehrenberg (2002). Probability misjudgment, cognitive ability, and belief in the paranormal. *British Journal of Psychology* 93: 169–177.

Myers, Frederic William Henry (1900). Presidential address. *Proceedings of the Society for Psychical Research* 37: 110–127.

Myers, Frederic William Henry (1903). *Human personality and its survival of bodily death* (Vol. 1 & 2). New York: Longmans, Green and Co.

Nash, Carroll (1958). Correlation between ESP and religious value. *The Journal of Parapsychology* 22: 204–209.

Nicol, Fraser (1966). Clerical contributions to parapsychology. *International Journal of Parapsychology* 8: 227–247.

Nisbett, Richard and Nancy Bellows (1977). Verbal reports about causal influences on social judgments: Private access versus public theories. *Journal of Personality and Social Psychology* 35: 613–624.

Northcote, Jeremy (2007). *The Paranormal and the Politics of Truth: A Sociological Account*. UK (Exeter): Imprint – Academic.

Oesterreich, Traugott Konstantin (1921). *Occultism and modern science (2ed.)*. London: Methuen and Co.

Oesterreich, Traugott Konstantin (1930). *Possession: demoniacal and other among primitive races, in antiquity, the middle ages, and modern times*. London: Kegan Paul.

Orenstein, Alan (2002). Religion and paranormal belief. *Journal for the Scientific Study of Religion* 41: 301–311.

Palmer, John (1979). A community mail survey of psychic experiences. *Journal of the American Society for Psychical Research* 73: 221–251.

Palmer, John and Brian Millar (2015). Experimenter effects in parapsychological research. In: *Parapsychology: a handbook for the 21st century*. Etzel Cardeña, John Palmer and David Marcussom-Clavertz (eds). North Caroline: McFarland & Company.

Paloutzian, Raymond and Crystal Park (2013). *Handbook for the Psychology of Religion and Spirituality (Second edition)*. New York: Guilford Press.

Pargament, Kenneth (2013). *APA Handbook of Psychology, Religion, and Spirituality* (Vol. 1 and 2). Washington, DC: American psychological Association.

Parker, Adrian (2000). A review of the Ganzfeld work at Gothenburg University. *Journal of the Society for Psychical Research* 64: 1–15.

Peltzer, Karl (2003). Magical thinking and paranormal beliefs among secondary and university students in South Africa. *Personality and Individual Differences* 35: 1419–1426.

Pence, David Evan (2020). How comparative psychology lost its soul: Psychical research and the new science of animal behavior. *Studies in history and philosophy of biological and biomedical sciences* 82: 101275.

Pennycook, Gordon, James Allan Cheyne, Paul Seli, Derek Koehler and Jonathan Fugelsang (2012). Analytic cognitive style predicts religious and paranormal belief. *Cognition* 123: 335–346.

Pennycook, Gordon, James Allan Cheyne, Nathaniel Barr, Derek Koehler and Jonathan Fugelsang (2015). On the reception and detection of pseudo-profound bullshit. *Judgement and Decision Making* 10: 549–563.

Pennycook, Gordon, Robert Ross, Derek Koehler and Jonathan Fugelsang (2016). Atheists and agnostics are more reflective than religious believers: Four empirical studies and a meta-analysis. *PLOS ONE* 11: e0153039.

Peres, Mario, Diego Swerts, Arão Belitardo de Oliveira, Frederico Camelo Leão, Alessandra Lamas Granero Lucchetti, Homero Vallada, Everton de Oliveira Maraldi, Rodrigo Toniol, Giancarlo Lucchetti (2020). Mental health and quality of life among adults with single, multiple, and no religious affiliations. *Journal of Nervous and Mental Disease* 208: 288–293.

Perry, Michael (1985). Understanding and explanation. In: *Parapsychology, philosophy, and religious concepts: proceedings of an international conference held in Rome, Italy*. Betty Shapin and Lisette Coly (eds). New York: Parapsychology Foundation, pp. 97–112.

Persinger, Michal and Katherine Makarec (1990). Exotic beliefs may be substitutes for religious beliefs. *Perceptual and Motor Skills* 71: 16–18.

Peters, Emmnauelle, Samantha Day, Jacqueline McKeena and Gilli Orbach (1999). Delusional ideation in religious and psychotic populations. *British Journal of Clinical Psychology* 38: 83–96.

Peters, Emmanuelle, Thomas Ward, Mike Jackson, Peter Woodruff, Craig Morgan, Philip McGuire and Philippa Garety (2017). Clinical relevance of appraisals of persistent psychotic experiences in people with and without a need for care: an experimental study. *The Lancet Psychiatry* 4: 927–936.

Podmore, Frank (1897). *Studies in Psychical Research*. New York: G. P. Putnam's Sons.

Podmore, Frank (1902). *Modern Spiritualism: a history and a criticism* (Vol. 1 & 2). London: Methuen & Co.

Porpora, Douglas (2006). Methodological atheism, methodological agnosticism, and religious experience. *Journal for the Theory of Social Behaviour* 36: 57–75.

Potts, Michael and Amy Devanno (2013). Tertualian's theory of the soul and contemporary psychical research. *Journal of the Society for Psychical Research* 77: 209–219.

Pratt, Joseph Gaiter, Ian Stevenson, William Roll, et al. (1968). Identification of Concealed Randomized Objects through Acquired Response Habits of Stimulus and Word Association. *Nature* 220: 89–91.

Rabeyron, Thomas and Caroline Watt (2010). Paranormal experiences, mental health and mental boundaries, and psi. *Personality and Individual Differences* 48: 487–492.

Radin, Dean (1997). *The conscious universe: the scientific truth of psychic phenomena.* New York: Harper Collins.

Radin, Dean (2006). *Entangled minds: extrasensory experiences in a quantum reality.* New York: Paraview Pocket Books.

Radin, Dean (2013). *Supernormal: science, yoga, and the evidence for extraordinary psychic abilities.* New York: Random House.

Radin, Dean (2018). *Real Magic: Ancient Wisdom, Modern Science, and a Guide to the Secret Power of the Universe.* New York: Random House.

Radin, Dean, Marilyn Schlitz and Christopher Baur (2015). Distant healing intention therapies: an overview of the scientific evidence. *Global Advances in Health Medicine* 4: 67–71.

Ramsey, Matthew, Steven Venette and Nicole Rabalais (2011). The Perceived Paranormal and Source Credibility: The Effects of Narrative Suggestions on Paranormal Belief. *Atlantic Journal of Communication* 19: 79–96.

Randi, James (1992). Help stamp out absurd beliefs. *Time* 139: 80.

Rao, Koneru Ramakrishna and John Palmer (1987). The anomaly called psi: recent research and criticism. *Behavioral and Brain Sciences* 10: 539–643.

Rawcliffe, D. H. (1959). *Illusions and delusions of the supernatural and the occult (The Psychology of the Occult).* New York: Dover Publications.

Reber, Arthur and James Alcock (2020). Searching for the Impossible: Parapsychology's Elusive Quest. *American Psychologist* 75: 391–399.

Reed, Graham (1988). *The psychology of anomalous experience.* Buffalo, NY: Prometheus Books.

Reuder, Mary (1999). A history of Division 36 (Psychology of Religion). In: *Unification through division: Histories of the divisions of the American Psychological Association,* Vol. 4. D. A. Dewsbury (ed.). Washington, DC: American Psychological Association, pp. 91–108.

Rhine, Joseph Banks (1934). *Extra-sensory perception.* Boston: Boston Society for Psychical Research.

Rhine, Joseph Banks (1950). Psi phenomena and psychiatry. *Proceedings of the Royal Society of Medicine* 43: 804–814.

Rhine, Joseph Banks (1953). *New World of the Mind*. New York: William Sloane.

Rhine, Joseph Banks (1985). The parapsychology of religion: a new branch of inquiry (Reprinted version of a paper originally published in 1977–1978 in the Journal of the Texas Society for Psychical Research). In: *Parapsychology, philosophy, and religious concepts: proceedings of an international conference held in Rome, Italy*. Betty Shapin and Lisette Coly (eds). New York: Parapsychology Foundation, pp. 191–215.

Rhine, Louisa (1965). *Hidden channels of the mind*. William Morrow.

Rice, Tom (2003). Believe it or not: religious and other paranormal beliefs in the united states. *Journal for the Scientific Study of Religion* 42: 95–106.

Riekki, Tapani, Marjaana Lindeman, Maria Aleneff, Anni Halme and Antti Nuortimo (2012a). Paranormal and Religious Believers Are More Prone to Illusory Face Perception than Skeptics and Non-believers. *Applied Cognitive Psychology* 27: 150–155.

Riekki, Tapani, Marjaana Lindeman and Jari Lipsanen (2013b). Conceptions about the mind-body problem and their relations to afterlife beliefs, paranormal beliefs, religiosity, and ontological confusions. *Advances in Cognitive Psychology* 9: 112–120.

Rock, Adam (2014). *The Survival Hypothesis: Essays on Mediumship*. Jefferson, North Carolina: McFarland and Company.

Rock, Adam, Julie Beischel and Christopher Cott (2009). Psi vs. survival: A qualitative investigation of mediums' phenomenology comparing psychic readings and ostensible communication with the deceased. *Transpersonal Psychology Review* 76–89.

Rock, Adam, Lance Storm, Harris Friedman (2012). Shamanic-like journeying and psi-signal detection: I. In search of the psi-conducive components of a novel experimental protocol. *The Journal of Parapsychology* 76: 321–326.

Roe, Christopher (1998b). Critical thinking and belief in the paranormal: a re-evaluation. *British Journal of Psychology* 90: 85–98.

Roe, Christopher (2020). Clinical parapsychology: the interface between anomalous experiences and psychological wellbeing. In: *Spirituality and Wellbeing: Interdisciplinary Approaches to the Study of Religious Experience and Health*. Bettina Schmidt and Jeff Leonardi (eds). Sheffield: Equinox Publishing Home, pp. 44–63.

Roig, Miguel, Robert Bridges, Catherine Hackett Renner, Cheryl Jackson (1998). Belief in the paranormal and its association with irrational thinking controlled for context effects. *Personality and Individual Differences* 24: 229–236.

Roiser, Jonathan, Oliver Howes, Christopher Chaddock, Eileen Joyce and Philip McGuire (2013). Neural and Behavioral Correlates of Aberrant Salience in Individuals at Risk for Psychosis. *Schizophrenia Bulletin* 39: 1328–1336.

Ross, Robert, Bjoern Hartig and Ryan McKay (2017). Analytic cognitive style predicts paranormal explanations of anomalous experiences but not the experiences themselves: Implications for cognitive theories of delusions. *Journal of Behavior Therapy and Experimental Psychiatry* 56: 90–96.

Roxburgh, Elizabeth and Christopher Roe (2011). A survey of dissociation, boundary thinness and psychological wellbeing of spiritualist mental mediumship. *The Journal of Parapsychology* 75: 279–300.

Royalty, Joel (1995). The generalizability of critical thinking: paranormal beliefs versus statistical reasoning. *The Journal of Genetic Psychology* 156: 477–488.

Sanchez, Clinton, Brian Sundermeier, Kenneth Gray and Robert Calin-Jageman (2017). Direct replication of Gervais & Norenzayan (2012): No evidence that analytic thinking decreases religious belief. *PLOS ONE* 12: e0172636.

Sass, Louis, Elizabeth Pienkos, Barnaby Nelson and Nick Medford (2013). Anomalous self-experience in depersonalization and schizophrenia: A comparative investigation. *Consciousness and Cognition* 22: 430–441.

Schiltz, Marylin, Richard Wiseman, Caroline Watt and Dean Radin (2006). Of two minds: sceptic proponent collaboration within parapsychology. *British Journal of Psychology* 97: 313–322.

Schmidt, Bettina (2017). Varieties of non-ordinary experiences in Brazil – a critical review of the contribution of studies of 'religious experience' to the study of religion. *International Journal of Latin-American Religions* 1:104–115.

Schofield, Kerry and Gordon Claridge (2007). Paranormal experiences and mental health: schizotypy as an underlyng factor. *Personality and Individual Differences* 43: 1908–1916.

Schofield, Malcolm, Ian Baker, Paul Staples and David Sheffield (2016). Mental Representations of the Supernatural: A Cluster Analysis of Religiosity, Spirituality and Paranormal Belief. *Personality and Individual Differences* 101: 419–424.

Schooler, Jonathan, Stephen Baumgart and Michael Franklin (2018). Entertaining without endorsing: The case for the scientific investigation of anomalous cognition. *Psychology of Consciousness: Theory, Research, and Practice* 5: 63–77.

Schultz, Duane and Sydney Ellen Schultz (2011). *A history of modern Psychology* (3rd Edition). Belmont, CA: Wadsworth.

Servadio, Emilio (1985). Mysticism and parapsychology. In: *Parapsychology, philosophy, and religious concepts: proceedings of an international conference held in Rome, Italy*. Betty Shapin and Lisette Coly (eds). New York: Parapsychology Foundation, pp. 2–19.

Schmeidler, Gertrude (1945). Separating the sheep from the goats. *Journal of the American Society for Psychical Research* 39: 47–49.

Shamdasani, Sonu (1994). Encountering Hélène: Théodore Flournoy and the genesis of subliminal psychology. In: *From India to the Planet Mars: a case of multiple personality with imaginary languages*. Théodore Flournoy. Princeton: Princeton University Press, pp. xi–li.

Shariff, Azim, Adam Cohen and Ara Norenzayan (2008). The Devil's Advocate: Secular Arguments Diminish both Implicit and Explicit Religious Belief. *Journal of Cognition and Culture* 8: 417–423.

Shenhav, Amitai, David Rand and Joshua Greene (2012). Divine intuition: Cognitive style influences belief in god. *Journal of Experimental Psychology: General* 141: 423–428.

Shermer, Michael (2002). *Why people believe weird things: pseudoscience, superstition, and other confusions of our time*. New York: Henry Holt and Company.

Shermer, Michael (2011). *The believing brain: from spiritual paths to political convictions – How we construct beliefs and reinforce them as truths*. London: Constable and Robinson.

Shushan, Gregory (2016). The sun told me I would be restored to life: Native American near-death experiences, shamanism, and religious revitalization movements. *Journal of Near-Death Studies* 34: 127–150.

Singer, Barry and Victor Benassi (1981). Occult beliefs: media distortions, social uncertainty, and deficiencies of human reasoning seem to be at the basis of occult beliefs. *American Scientist* 69: 49–55.

Smith, Matthew, Christa Foster and Gordon Stovin (1998). Intelligence and paranormal belief: Examining the role of context. *The Journal of Parapsychology* 62, 65–77.

Society for Psychical Research (1885). Report of the committee appointed to investigate phenomena connected with the Theosophical society. *Proceedings of the Society for Psychical Research* 3: 201–207.

Sommer, Andreas (2012). Psychical research and the origins of American psychology: Hugo Münsterberg, William James and Eusapia Palladino. *History of the Human Sciences* 25: 23–44.

Sparks, Glenn, Marianne Pellechia and Chris Irvine (1998) Does television news about UFOs affect viewers' UFO beliefs? An experimental investigation. *Communication Quarterly* 46: 284–294.

Sparks, Glenn (2001). The relationship between paranormal beliefs and religious beliefs. *Skeptical Inquirer* 18: 386–395.

Spitz, Herman (1997). *Nonconscious movements: from mystical messages to facilitated communication*. New Jersey: Lawrence Erlbaum Associates.

Spilka, Bernard and Kevin Ladd (2013). *The Psychology of Prayer: a scientific approach*. New York: The Guilford Press.

Stagnaro, Michael, Robert Ross, Gordon Pennycook, David Rand (2019). Cross-cultural support for a link between analytic thinking and disbelief in God: Evidence from India and the United Kingdom. *Judgment and Decision Making* 14: 179–186.

Stanford, Rex (1974). An experimentally testable model for spontaneous psi events: I. Extrasensory events. *Journal of the American Society for Psychical Research* 68: 34–57.

Stanford, Rex (2015). Psychological concepts of psi function: A review and constructive critique. In: *Parapsychology: A handbook for the 21st century*. Etzel Cardeña, John Palmer and David Marcusson-Clavertz (eds). McFarland & Co., pp. 94–109.

Stark, Rodney and William Sims Bainbridge (1986). *The Future of Religion*. Berkeley: University of California Press.

Stevenson, Ian (1977). Research into the evidence of man's survival after death: a historical and critical survey with a summary of recent developments. *The Journal of Nervous and Mental Disease* 165: 152–170.

Stevenson, Ian (1980). *Twenty Cases Suggestive of Reincarnation (3rd edition)*. Virginia: University Press of Virginia. (Original work published in 1966).

Storm, Lance and Michael Thalbourne (1998–1999). The Transliminal Connection Between Paranormal Effects and Personality in an Experiment with the I Ching. *European Journal of Parapsychology* 14: 100–124.

Streib, Heinz, Constantin Klein, Barbara Keller and Ralph Wilbur Hood Jr. (2020). The Mysticism Scale as Measure for Subjective Spirituality: New Results with Hood's M-Scale and the Development of a Short Form. In: *Assessing Spirituality in a Diverse World*. Amy L. Al., Paul Wink, Raymond F. Paloutzian and Kevin A. Harris (eds). New York: Springer, pp. 467–491.

Streib, Heinz, Zhuo Chen and Ralph Wilbur Hood Jr. (2020). Categorizing People by Their Preference for Religious Styles. *International Journal for the Psychology of Religion* 30: 112–127.

Sudre, René (1956). *Traité de Parapsychologie*. Paris: Payot.

Surbhi, Khanna and Bruce Greyson (2015). Near-Death Experiences and Posttraumatic Growth. *Journal of Nervous and Mental Disease* 203: 749–755.

Svedholm, Annika and Marjaana Lindeman (2018). The separate roles of the reflective mind and involuntary inhibitory control in gatekeeping paranormal beliefs and the underlying intuitive confusions. *British Journal of Psychology* 104: 303–319.

Tam, Wai-cheong Carl and Yung-Jong Shiah (2004). Paranormal belief, religiosity and cognitive complexity. *Proceedings of the 47th Parapsychological Association Convention at Vienna, Austria*, pp. 423–429.

Tanner, Amy (1910). *Studies in Spiritism*. New York: Appleton.

Targ, Russell and Harold Puthoff (1974). Information transmission under conditions of sensory shielding. *Nature* 251: 602–607.

Tart, Charles (2002). Parapsychology and transpersonal psychology: anomalies to be explained away or spirit to manifest? *The Journal of Parapsychology* 66: 31–47.

Tart, Charles (2003). Spiritual motivations of parapsychologists? Empirical data *The Journal of Parapsychology* 67: 181–184.

Tart, Charles (2009). *The end of materialism: how evidence of the paranormal is bringing science and spirit together*. New Harbinger Publications.

Taves, Ann (2009). *Religious experience reconsidered: a building-block approach to the study of religion and other special things*. Princeton: Princeton University Press.

Taves, Ann (2014). A tale of two congresses: the psychological study of psychical, occult, and religious phenomena, 1900–1909. *Journal of the History of the Behavioral Sciences* 50: 376–399.

Taves, Ann (2016). *Revelatory events: three case studies of the emergence of new spiritual paths*. Princeton: Princeton University Press.

Taves, Ann (2020). Mystical and Other Alterations in Sense of Self: An Expanded Framework for Studying Nonordinary Experiences. *Perspectives on Psychological Science* 15: 669–690.

Taves, Ann, Melissa Gordon Wolf, Elliott D. Ihm, Michael Barlev, Michael Kinsella and Maharshi Vyas (2019). What Counts as Religious Experience? the Inventory of Nonordinary Experiences as a Tool for Analysis Across Cultures. *PsyArXiv* December 28. doi:10.31234/osf.io/ux28d.

Thalbourne, Michael (1991). The psychology of mystical experience. *Exceptional Human Experience* 9: 168–186.

Transliminality Michael (1998). Transliminality: further correlates and a short measure. *Journal of the American Society for Psychical Research* 92: 402–419.

Thalbourne, Michael (2000a). Transliminality: a review. *International Journal of Parapsychology* 11: 1–34.

Thalbourne, Michael (2000b). Transliminality and creativity. *Journal of Creative Behavior* 34: 193–202.

Thalbourne, Michael (2002). Religiosity/spirituality and belief in the paranormal: a German replication. *Journal of the Society for Psychical Research* 66: 113–114.

Thalbourne, Michael (2003a). *A glossary of terms used in parapsychology*. Charlottesville, Virginia: Puente Publications.

Thalbourne, Michael (2003b). Theism and belief in the paranormal. *Journal of the Society for Psychical Research* 67: 208–210.

Thalbourne, Michael (2009). Transliminality, anomalous belief and experience, and hypnotizability. *Australian Journal of Clinical and Experimental Hypnosis* 37: 119–130.

Thalbourne, Michael and Rebecca O'Brien (1999). Belief in the paranormal and religious variables. *Journal of the Society for Psychical Research* 63: 110–122.

Thalbourne, Michael, James Houran, Susan Crawley (2003). Childhood trauma as a possible antecedent of transliminality. *Psychological Reports* 93: 687–694.

Thalbourne, Michael and Oriana Nofi (1997). Belief in the paranormal, superstitiousness and intellectual ability. *Journal of the Society for Psychical Research* 61: 365–371.

Thalbourne, Michael, Luciana Bartemucci, Peter Delin, Bronwyn Fox and Oriana Nofi (1997). Transliminality: its nature and correlates. *Journal of the American Society for Psychical Research* 91: 305–331.

Thalbourne, Michael, Susan Crawley and James Houran (2003). Temporal lobe lability in the highly transliminal mind. *Personality and Individual Differences* 35: 1965–1974.

Thalbourne, Michael A. and John Maltby (2008). Transliminality, thin boundaries, unusual experiences, and temporal lobe lability. *Personality and Individual Differences* 44: 1617–1623.

Thalbourne, Michael and Peter Delin (1994). A common thread underlying belief in the paranormal, creative personality, mystical experience and psychopathology *The Journal of Parapsychology* 58: 3–38.

Thalbourne, Michale and Peter Delin (1999). Transliminality: its relation to dream life, religiosity and mystical experience. *International Journal for the Psychology of Religion* 9(1): 45–61.

Thouless, Robert (1971). *An introduction to the psychology of religion (3ed.)*. Cambridge: Cambridge University Press.

Thurston, Herbert (1933). *The church and Spiritualism*. Milwaukee: The Bruce Publishing Company.

Thurston, Herbert (1952). *The Physical Phenomena of Mysticism* (J. C. Crehan, ed.). London: Burns Oates.

Tobacyk, Jerome (1983a). Death threat, death concerns and paranormal belief. *Death Studies* 7:115–124.

Tobacyk, Jerome (1983b). Reduction in paranormal belief among participants in a college course. *Skeptical Inquirer* 8: 57–61.

Tobacyk, Jerome (2004). A revised Paranormal Belief Scale. *The International Journal of Transpersonal Studies* 23: 94–98.

Tobacyk, Jerome, Mark Miller and Glenda Jones (1984). Paranormal beliefs of high school students. *Psychological Reports* 55: 255–261.

Ullman, Montague and Stanley Krippner (1970). An Experimental Approach to Dreams and Telepathy: II. Report of Three Studies. *American Journal of Psychiatry* 126: 1282–1289.

Utts, Jessica (1991). Replication and meta-analysis in parapsychology. *Statistical Science* 6: 363–403.

van Elk, Michiel (2015). Perceptual Biases in Relation to Paranormal and Conspiracy Beliefs. *PLOS ONE* 10: e0130422.

Walach, Harald (2015). *Secular Spirituality: The Next Step Towards Enlightenment*. New York: Springer.

Walach, Harald, Niko Kohls, Nikolaus von Stillfried, Thilo Hinterberger and Stefan Schmidt (2009). Spirituality: the legacy of parapsychology. *Archive for the Psychology of Religion* 31: 277–308.

Watson, Paul (2019). Psychology and Religion within an ideological surround. *Religion and Psychology* 1: 1–89.

Watt, Caroline and Richard Wiseman (2002). Experimenter differences in cognitive correlates of paranormal belief and psi. *The Journal of Parapsychology* 66: 371–385.

Wesp, Richard and Kathleen Montgomery (1998). Developing critical thinking through the study of paranormal phenomena. *Teaching of Psychology* 25: 275–278.

White, Rhea (1985). Meaning, metanoia, and psi. In: *Parapsychology, philosophy, and religious concepts: proceedings of an international conference held in Rome, Italy.* Betty Shapin and Lisette Coly (eds). New York: Parapsychology Foundation, pp. 167–190.

White, Rhea (1997). Dissociation, narrative, and exceptional human experiences. In: *Broken images, broken selves: dissociative narratives in clinical practice.* Stanley Krippner and Susan Marie Powers (eds). Washington, DC: Brunner/Mazel, pp. 88–121.

Wierzbicki, Michael (1985). Reasoning errors and belief in the paranormal. *Journal of Social Psychology* 125: 489–494.

Williams, Emyr, Leslie Francis and Christopher Lewis (2009). Introducing the Modified Paranormal Belief Scale: Distinguishing Between Classic Paranormal Beliefs, Religious Paranormal Beliefs and Conventional Religiosity Among Undergraduates in Northern Ireland and Wales. *Archive for the Psychology of Religion* 31: 345–356.

Wiseman, Richard and Marilyn Schlitz (1997). Experimenter effects and the remote detection of staring. *The Journal of Parapsychology* 61: 197–207.

Wiseman, Richard and Caroline Watt (2006). Belief in psychic ability and the misattribution hypothesis: a qualitative review. *British Journal of Psychology* 97: 323–338.

Wiseman, Richard, Caroline Watt, Diana Kornbrot (2019). Registered reports: an early example and analysis. *PeerJ* 7: e6232.

Wolfradt, Uwe, Viktor Oubaid, Eckart Straube, Natascha Bischoff and Johannes Mischo (1999). Thinking styles, schizotypal traits and anomalous experiences. *Personality and Individual Differences* 27: 821–830.

Wright, John Stafford (1955). Making sense of parapsychology. *The Churchman* 69: 84–89.

Wulff, David (1991). *Psychology of religion: classic and contemporary views.* New York: John Wiley & Sons.

Wulff, David (2014). Mystical experiences. In: *Varieties of anomalous experience: Examining the scientific evidence*, 2nd ed. Etzel Cardeña, Steven Jay Lynn and Stanley Krippner (eds). Washington, DC: American Psychological Association, pp. 369–408.

Wüsten, Caroline, Björn Schlier, Edo Jaya, Eduardo Fonseca-Pedrero, Emmanuelle Peters, Hélène Verdoux, Todd Woodward, Tim Ziermans and Tania Lincoln (2018). Psychotic experiences and related distress: A cross-national comparison and network analysis based on 7141 participants from 13 countries. *Schizophrenia Bulletin* 44: 1185–1194.

Wuthnow, Robert (1978). *Experimentation in American religion: the new mysticisms and their implications for the churches.* Berkeley, CA: University of California Press.

Žeželj, Iris and Lilijana Lazarević (2019). Irrational beliefs. *Europe's Journal of Psychology* 15: 1–7.

Zorab, George (1957). ESP experiments with psychotics. *Journal of the American Society for Psychical Research* 39: 162–164.

Zuckerman, Phil, Luke Galen and Frank Pasquale (2016). *The nonreligious: understanding secular people and societies.* New York: Oxford University Press.

Zusne, Leonard and Warren Jones (1989). *Anomalistic psychology: A study of magical thinking* (2nd ed.). New York, NY: Erlbaum.

Index